# Assumptions

## That Affect Our Lives

The Shaping of Western Civilization
A Contrast Between Greek and Hebrew Thought

Christian Overman

Micah Publishing

*Presents*

Assumptions That Affect Our Lives
© 1996 by Christian Overman

International Standard Book Number

0-9714532-7-6

Printed in the United States of America

Micah Publishing is a division of the Charleston Publishing Group
of P.O. Box 54, Louisiana, Missouri 63353

04 05 06 — 6 5 4 3 2

*Dedicated to:*

## Dr. Albert E. Greene, Jr.

With sincere gratitude
and deep appreciation

# Acknowledgements

I am especially grateful for the encouragement of Gary and Anne Marie Ezzo, of Growing Families International, who believed the work warranted republication, and to Jim Waller, of Lifeline Resources, for his steady support. In addition, I am indebted to the late Dr. Dan Pecota, of Northwest College, and to Diana Waring for their thoughtful review of the manuscript and many helpful comments. With regards to readability, you all have my wife, Kathy, to thank. She kept me alert to the fact that it was supposed to be understandable to the man on the street, and her encouraging words kept me going with this goal in mind.

A special word of thanks goes to Don Johnson, director of the Biblical Worldview Institute and superintendent of the Cascade Christian School District in Puyallup, Washington, who granted permission for reprinting the excerpt from *Making the Connections* in Chapter Eight.

# Table of Contents

# Preface

W hatever happened to ancient Greece? What can we learn from that civilization? Whatever happened to ancient Israel, its history, poetry and traditions? What can we learn from them?

When a business or an organization shows signs of decline, an outside consultant is sometimes brought in to help. Why? Because the people who live and work within a particular industry become so accustomed to the way things are, they lose sight of the way things really should be. A good advisor, then, looks at the problems from a different angle, and helps those within an organization to see things from a fresh perspective. As a result, when old problems are approached with new insights, creative energies are revived and positive results occur.

We currently live in a culture in decline, and moral regression is a recognized sign of our times. If we are to see a reversal in the downward trend we have experienced over the past forty years, it would help if we could gain a fresh perspective on ourselves and the problems which surround us. To stand back and see our condition from a different angle is an important step in reviving our health. This book attempts to do just that, to step back and look at the foundational assumptions that currently guide our culture – assumptions that go all the way back to ancient Greece.

The similarities between our culture and that of ancient Greece during its later stages of decay are many and sobering. Apart from a broad-based reformation of thought and action, I believe our society will continue its moral descent like decadent Greece did some 2,400 years ago. But looking at what we should not do is no solution. We must examine what we should do and why.

This book was written with the belief that a reversal of our current moral decline is possible, and the keys to such a change are found in an ancient Hebraic Book. By viewing our present situation through the eyes of the ancients, not only will we be better able to see the issues for what they are, but also understand what must be done to effect change. And change we must.

Since the term "Hebrew model" appears throughout this writing, a word of clarification is necessary. First, and most important, the Hebrew model refers to the model of thought, given by the inspiration of God, which we call the Bible – both Old and New Testaments – written almost entirely by Hebrews. The Word of God enables man to understand who he is, why he is, and how he is to relate to others. More importantly, it tells us who God is.

Second, the term Hebrew model refers to the model of the nation of ancient Israel itself. However, this aspect of the Hebrew model (that is, the way they actually lived) was not always in harmony with the model of God's Word. Sometimes the model of the ancient Hebrews demonstrates what we should do, and at other times it demonstrates what we should not do. In either case, whether positive or negative, their experience is a model, an example from which we are to learn.

As a people chosen to be a God-honoring culture in a pagan world, the Hebrews bore a great responsibility. They were chosen to be a distinctive culture in which the ways of God were applied throughout all of life: in their families, their jobs, their economy, and their government. They were to be an example to other nations of the blessings which come when a culture loves God, and they were also an example of what happens when God is forgotten. Their "chosenness" was not so much a matter of special preference or privilege, but rather of special obligation. In this sense, they were to the ancient world what the church is to today's world: "a chosen race, a royal priesthood, a holy nation, a people for God's own possession," for the purposes of proclaiming His excellence in the earth (see 1 Peter 2:9; Exodus 19:5-6).

Yet just as in the Body of Christ today we have various actions of men which cloud the clear message of what a God-honoring people should be, some Hebrews developed their own traditions which led them down the road of dead religion, emphasizing the letter of the Law and neglecting its spirit. Such aspects of Hebrew custom are to be set aside, even as Paul admonished Titus to pay no attention to "Jewish myths and commandments of men who turn away from the truth," (Titus 1:14). In this respect, the term Hebrew model, as used in this writing, may not always represent "Jewish thinking" per se, or Jewish practice, whether past or present.

Even so, Christians must realize that the biblical foundation stones of Israel are also their own. It is important to dust them off and view them afresh from the perspective of the ancient Hebrew, so we can more effectively enter into the cultural transformation necessary in exchanging our Western, Greek foundations of thought for different stones upon which to build. For we all have a great deal of remodeling to do.

Christian Overman, M. Ed.
Executive Director, Worldview Matters
"Think Again!" Workshops
Bellevue, Washington

# Chapter One

# From Athens and Jerusalem

A n American bomber with a crew of seven men took off from an air base in North Africa during World War II, to drop its payload of bombs over Naples, Italy. When the mission was complete, the plane and its crew headed for home base, but never arrived. For many years the fate of the Lady Be Good remained a mystery. It was thought the plane had run out of fuel, and crashed in the Mediterranean Sea. But in reality, it had plenty of fuel. Enough to fly 442 miles past its destination to where it was found 17 years later, ditched in the Sahara desert.

What happened? On that night, an unusually strong tail wind caused the bomber and its crew to reach the coast of North Africa hours ahead of schedule. When their flight instruments indicated they had flown far enough, they just could not believe it. They assumed it was simply impossible to fly that great a distance in so short a time. Coming to the conclusion the enemy was jamming their instruments, or the instruments were just malfunctioning, the officer in charge made a decision to continue. It was a decision that cost the crew their lives.

Our circumstances may not seem as dramatic as that of the bomber's crew, but the principle is the same for us as it was for them: behind important decisions are some even more important underlying assumptions.

This book is about the assumptions we make, and how those assumptions affect our lives. Assumptions mold our way of thinking, shape our conclusions, and direct the decisions that lie behind our actions and attitudes. They affect decisions on how we relate to others, and with whom we spend our time. Decisions on how we vote, as well as decisions on how we dress. Moral decisions. Marriage decisions. Retirement decisions. You name it. They're all based on underlying assumptions.

The amazing thing is, the "assumption" part of our decision-making process is usually the part that gets the least examination. Often, it's the part we don't think much about at all. It's the part we take for granted. We accept it as a "given" because it just doesn't seem possible it could be any other way, like the crew on the bomber who believed it just was not possible for a plane to fly that far that fast, and went on to draw conclusions from that assumption.

Few of us take the time to question our assumptions. Yet, they have a tremendous effect upon the way we live and act. What's more, we continue to live and act in certain ways until such time we become convinced our assumptions are in need of a change. But once our assumptions are corrected, the change of course comes easily.

We often underestimate the importance of unspoken assumptions behind the spoken words and visible actions of those around us. Like an iceberg floating on the ocean with just ten percent of it visible above the waves and ninety percent of it below the surface, we sometimes lose sight of the fact that the words we hear and read, and the actions we see from others, are first shaped by invisible thoughts, deep in the unseen world of a person's heart.

It's easy to see how an individual's assumptions can affect the decisions he or she makes. But assumptions not only affect individuals, they also affect whole societies.

Some years ago an American couple was traveling through a remote part of South Africa when they came across an unusual sight. Before them lay a village with the most remarkable architecture. What was so different about it was the fact that each and every hut was exactly the same. Not only were they all round, with a pointed top, but each one was mathematically identical to the very inch, without the slightest variation.

The travelers came upon a family building a new hut. Here again, the dimensions of the house were exactly that of their neighbors'. Why? There was a reason. You see, this particular tribe held to a basic assumption that it was morally wrong for one man to have more than another. Hence, every man's home was equal in size and shape, no matter how many people needed to live there. This cultural assumption was so strongly held that anyone who made a larger hut could be expelled from the tribe, or perhaps murdered. The assumption affected much more than their building codes. It permeated their entire way of life, and explained why even their clothing was not hung in public to dry.

What about our own society? Are there some deeply-held, taken-for-granted assumptions which directly influence and guide the way we think, live, work and play? The answer is, yes. In this book we want to take a closer look at some of those cultural assumptions which form the foundation of our society – some of which you may never have thought much about.

Cultural assumptions are like the ground-level foundation of a house, a very important part of the home, but not often visited. When was the last time you crawled under your house to look at the foundation? Maybe you've never seen the foundation of your home. You just assume it is there, doing what it is supposed to be doing – holding up the house.

What we want to do in this book is to get out our flashlights and go under the crawl space of our culture, so to speak, and take a second look (or maybe even a first look) at what beliefs are holding it up. Our purpose is to discover why we act the way we do, and why other people act the way they do. We will find that people act differently because their thoughts are rooted in different assumptions, causing them to view the world through different windows. If we look closely enough, we will discover there is a reason behind the actions and attitudes of people we read about in the newspaper, talk to on the phone, and, most importantly, see in the mirror. And if we are going to be wise in our understanding of the times in which we live, we must get down to the assumption level of human behavior.

## CULTURAL ASSUMPTIONS: WHERE DID THEY COME FROM?

The bride and groom stand before the altar as the minister asks, "What token do you give as a symbol of your love?" "This ring," comes the reply. On cue, the ring bearer steps forward to present the golden band. The groom reaches over, takes the ring with one hand, holds the left hand of his bride with the other, and ever so gently slips the eternal circle over her delicate third finger. It is easy to understand why people wear wedding rings. Besides being a reminder of one's vows, and a symbol of one's love, the presence of the wedding band also tells others a man or a woman is spoken for. But why is the ring worn on the left hand? And why the third finger?

If you research the matter, you will discover the custom goes back to the Romans. They believed a small artery, called *vena amoris*, or the "vein of love," ran from the third finger to the heart. It was felt wearing a ring on this finger joined the hearts of the couple in their destiny. The left hand was selected because it was closer to the heart.

Cultural habits don't just come out of nowhere. Even if the people who practice them have forgotten why they do it, you can be sure their customs had a starting point in history. Although cultural habits often change over time, they do have original roots. For those of us who live in what is known as the "Western" world, our cultural roots go back primarily to two historic starting points: the ancient Greeks and the ancient Hebrews. This is not to say we couldn't go back further. But for the purposes of this discussion, we will focus primarily on the Hebrews and the Greeks because they have so strongly impacted our Western ways of thinking, right up to the present hour.

Since the fifth century B.C., Greek ways of thinking have infiltrated Europe and the Western world. Even the Romans took most of their cultural cues from the Greeks who came before them. It was the Greeks who first laid in place certain cornerstones of Western culture, shaping our ground rules for philosophy, science, politics, and education, as well as competitive sports and the creative arts.

Culturally speaking, we are swimming in Greek soup, surrounded and immersed in ways of seeing and doing which date back to ideas planted and cultivated over a period of about three hundred years (600-300 B.C.) by such thinkers as Thales, Anaximander, Socrates, Plato, Aristotle, and others who left their fingerprints unquestionably behind, as we'll see clearly in later chapters.

As for the ancient Hebrews, their imprint upon the West is deep and far-reaching as well. Our concepts of morality, law, and ethics are unmistakably rooted in the Bible, which is a distinctly Hebrew book. Justice, virtue, right and wrong, good and evil – such terms carry particular meanings to Westerners because of definitions going back to Moses and Mt. Sinai, and underscored throughout the entire Scripture, including the New Testament, which is a Hebraic writing as well.

To say the Bible is "Hebraic," both Old Testament and New, is to say its human authors (with the exception of Luke) were Jewish through and through. The Bible was written by sons of Abraham, Isaac, and Jacob, who grew up, lived, and died in a peculiar culture having unique customs and assumptions which set them dramatically apart from their neighbors in a host of ways. Hebraic thought patterns were radically different from those of the Greeks. So much so, the ancient Hebrews would not tolerate the study of Greek philosophy in their schools.

In the Talmud, the collection of ancient writings of rabbis which provides the basis of authority for orthodox Judaism, we are told of a young man who wanted to study "Greek wisdom." He went to his uncle, a rabbi, with his request. The uncle reminded him of Joshua 1:8, which speaks of meditating on God's Word day and night. "Go then," said the wise rabbi, "and find a time that is neither day or night, and learn then Greek wisdom." (Menachot 99b).

This story illustrates the seriousness of the conflict between Greek and Hebrew thought. It produced a difference of culture so strong the early historian Tertullian asked, "What has Athens to do with Jerusalem?" The implied answer, of course, was "Nothing." Culturally speaking, the Hebrews were swimming in a much different kind of soup than Socrates. The Bible reflects this difference from cover to cover.

There is another sense, however, in which we can rightly say the Bible is not a Hebrew book at all. Its actual author is neither Hebrew nor Greek, but God Himself. This is why we often refer to it as "God's Word," in recognition of the source of the Scripture's inspiration. In an ultimate sense, then, the Bible is not the product of any culture, Jewish or otherwise. But what we must clearly understand is, although God did inspire the Scriptures, He did not bypass the human vessels through which the message came. In a very practical way, God chose to communicate His message via human language and thought as spoken and understood by the everyday people with whom He wanted to communicate. People who lived in a particular culture, who understood certain ways of thought, and subscribed to certain customs. In other words, while the Bible did not come from Hebraic culture, it did come through it.

The fact God chose a particular group of people through which to communicate His Word does not lessen the truth of divine inspiration. Nor does it negate the fact that the message is intended for all men of every culture. Think of it this way: since the message first came to the Jews, the only thoughtful thing for God to do was to speak in a way which made sense to them. Our job, then, is to bear this in mind and read God's Word accordingly. If we are going to understand the Bible as fully and clearly as possible, we would do well to read it through the eyes and understanding of ancient Hebrew culture and custom – ways which often stand in as much contrast to us as they did to the ancient Greek. Perhaps some examples will help at this point.

### THE DIFFERENCE BETWEEN GREEK AND HEBREW THOUGHT

John and Martha, that young couple we saw standing at the altar earlier in this chapter, were hopelessly in love. During the ceremony, while the soloist was singing "I Love You Truly," the two lovers seemed to be totally lost in a world of their own. While not trying to eavesdrop, the minister couldn't help but overhear them faintly whisper as they gazed into each other's eyes:

John: "My darling, your belly is like a heap of wheat!"
Martha: "Oh, my love, you say the kindest things!"

Sound a bit strange? It wouldn't have sounded strange to Solomon, or to the maiden to whom he spoke these very words some 3,000 years ago, as we read in the Song of Solomon, chapter 7, verse 2. But if you imagine Solomon's lover having a big, round stomach, you are experiencing your Greek mind at work.

There is something in our Greek way of thinking which longs for photographic impressions. Please do not misunderstand this, or carry things too far. There is nothing wrong with photographic images. The point is simply this: for us, as for the ancient Greek, a primary emphasis is placed upon how things are experienced by the human eye.

The Greeks, for example, were great pioneers in three dimensional sculpture. Their architectural designs stand today as classical wonders, having columns sometimes built wider at the top and tapering down to the bottom, or at times wider toward the middle, for no practical reason, but simply making the appearance more appealing to the senses.

If you read their literature, such as Homer's *Iliad* or *Odyssey,* you will often find vivid images, full of color and detail, like a motion picture. The ocean is described as "wine-blue water," for example, and the story of Odysseus building his raft describes him trimming tall trees with a bronze ax having an olive wood handle, and using a chalk line to plane the planks truly straight.

For the Hebrews, on the other hand, what is of primary concern is the essence of things. For them, content came first, while external form came second. For example, in the description of Noah's ark we are given the name of a type of wood used, the ark's length, width, and height, the fact it had a window opening around the top, a door in the side, and an internal construction of three levels. In short, we're given to know the ark as a wooden, watertight vessel having a means of fresh air circulation and being large enough to hold its necessary cargo.

The essence of the matter is, this boat was big, seaworthy, and fully functional. A visual detail of the ship's form is not given, however. Did it have a pointed bow, a rounded bow, or a square bow like a barge? Was the roof flat or inclined? If inclined, was it a gentle slope, or a steep one? Nor is there any description of the tools Noah used, or the manner in which he did his work. There is no mention of the color of the flood waters, even though "dirty brown" would probably have been very appropriate.

Does this mean color and visual impressions were unimportant to the Hebrews? Of course not. Color and form were sometimes of great importance, especially when they carried with them some essential meaning or significance, such as in the various materials and pieces of furniture used in the tabernacle in the wilderness. It so happens, however, that color and visual impact are not essential to the meaning and significance of the ark and its message.

This tendency to view the world through the window of "essence" is often seen in the Bible's descriptions of people. Other than to say a particular person was beautiful (such as Esther) or handsome (such as David) or having "no comeliness" (such as the Messiah), the Scriptures do not often provide physical details. It is significant to note that in all four Gospel accounts of the life of Christ, not one author provides a physical description of Jesus. Think about this for a moment. If you had written one of the Gospels yourself, wouldn't you have given at least a brief description of the Lord's physical attributes? The fact is, we don't even know if He was tall or short. Yet, we have a craving to know how He appeared, as evidenced by the many paintings of Christ our various artists have done, as they imagine Him to have looked.

The primary focus of attention upon Jesus in the Bible is on His thought, speech, and interaction with others. The essence of His being is the focal point.

His internal qualities, rather than His external shape. His "content" rather than His "form." This, then, explains the mystery of Solomon's strange sounding words to the young maiden, when he said, "Your belly is like a heap of wheat." We must read and understand these words in terms of their essence and internal characteristics (or content) rather than in terms of a photographic image or description of external form. Solomon's description of her belly was not how she appeared to the eye, but what she evoked in his soul.

What is the essence of a heap of wheat? Its essence speaks of abundant fruitfulness and bountiful harvest. In terms of the qualities of a young woman, it would communicate the hope of bearing many children, something of great value to a Middle Eastern man. Looking further into Solomon's "language of love," you will find more unusual descriptions. Take this line, for example: "Your nose is like the tower of Lebanon, which looks toward Damascus." Or this one: "Your neck is like the tower of David, built for an armory [a storehouse for military weapons!], on which hang a thousand bucklers, all shields of mighty men." What on earth could he possibly be trying to communicate to her? With lines like this, you might seriously question Solomon's wisdom, if you did not understand his mode of thought.

The essence of his words have a lot to do with the idea that this young woman was no ordinary girl. Maybe she did have a large nose, but this is not the essence of his message. Here we have a woman fit to be a queen. Steady, stately, solid and sure, she towered above the crowd in comparison. Furthermore, we see a woman who brought out the core of Solomon's masculinity, like the smell of battle to a warrior. No doubt, she was something he wanted to conquer. She was as great a prize to him as David's storehouse of armor for a thousand soldiers in time of war. She was a challenge this ancient Romeo-King couldn't pass up. A trophy beyond all others.

Such contrasts between Greek and Hebrew thought have fascinated scholars and historians for centuries. Some even feel the Hebrews and Greeks viewed time differently. The Greeks, for example, are thought to have viewed history as a never-ending cycle of aimless repetition. People were born, lived their lives, and died, as more people followed behind who did the same. Houses were newly built, deteriorated through time, and were replaced with new ones that did the same. Plants and animals all went through the same cycle, and history went in circles, repeating itself with no destination in sight.

The Hebrews, on the other hand, viewed human history as going somewhere. It had a definite beginning and was headed toward a definite goal, culminating in the messianic reign of Israel's Redeemer. Theirs was a straight line concept of history, moving ahead like an arrow to its target.

The aim of this book, however, is not to discuss the subtle differences between Greek and Hebrew thought. We will leave this for the scholars to debate. Instead, we will direct our attention to major points of difference which caused ancient Hebrews and Greeks to think and act so contrarily to one another. We will be looking at the foundational assumptions which shaped the different ways they treated one another, reared their children, did their work, and worshipped. And as we move along in our search, we will be asking questions, making observations, and drawing parallels between the ancients and ourselves.

We will be comparing our own beliefs with theirs, discovering similarities and differences, with the goal in mind of understanding more clearly the striking differences between biblical and nonbiblical thinking. By the time we are through, we should all have a better understanding of what our basic assumptions should be as Bible-believing Christians, and hopefully see more clearly what it means to think biblically in a predominately anti-biblical culture like the one in which we currently live.

### THE CHRISTIAN MIND AND GREEK THOUGHT

Take this short history quiz. What time and place in history do the following statements describe?

- People, especially the educated ones, have rejected traditional religion.
- Cults from the East have been accepted.
- Astrology is practiced.
- Patriotism has declined.
- Men practice manners which have previously been considered effeminate.
- The upper class is consumed with the pursuit of pleasure.
- Education stresses knowledge more than character, and produces masses of half-educated people.
- Public athletic games have turned into professional contests.
- Homosexuality is popular.

- Men who want to watch dances by unclad women do not have to go far to find them.
- The dramas of the day are full of seduction and adultery.
- A women's liberation movement has brought women into active roles in a culture which has previously been male oriented.
- Motherhood is devalued, and the bearing of children is viewed as an inconvenience.
- Abortion is commonly practiced, as well as infanticide.

Choose the best answer from the following:
A. America, during the 1950s
B. Ancient Greece, during the later stages of its decline
C. America, today

(If you selected B or C, you are correct. Either one will do.)

The similarities between decadent Greece and present day America are stark and sobering. Even more sobering is the fact that many of these descriptions so fitting for today would have been unthinkable in the 1950s, just 50 years earlier. We've come a long way in a short time. The descriptions of ancient Greece listed above are those given by historian Will Durant in his well-known book, *The Life of Greece*, published in 1939.[1] He writes about these characteristics of Greek culture near the latter part of the book, in a subsection entitled, "The Morals of Decay." This was Greece near the end of her life.

Some readers may question the inclusion of infanticide as a distinctive mark of American culture today. But in the year 2000, America's likeness to dying Greece was made complete when the United States Supreme Court overturned a Nebraska State law prohibiting so-called "partial birth abortion." This procedure is nothing less than blatant infanticide, in its cruelest and most painful form. It embraces the pagan assumption that the lives of certain children are better left unlived. Even as far back as 1973, Nobel Prize-winner Dr. James D. Watson urged, "If a child were not declared alive until three days after birth, then all parents could be allowed the choice that only a few are given under the present system. The doctor could allow the child to die if the parents so chose and save a lot of misery and suffering."[2] Dr. Watson's suggestion is one up on the ancient Greeks. In Athens, parents were given ten days to decide whether or not to accept a newborn into the family.

When it came to the matter of abortions in Athens, the physicians did not perform them because The Hippocratic Oath of medical ethics would not allow such practice. It was the Greek midwife who became the experienced hand, and no law impeded her.[3] But no such medical ethics impede a modern doctor's work. Yes, we have come a very long way in a very short time, and in this respect we have surpassed the Greeks in our moral decline.

Remember the lesson of the Lady Be Good, the World War II bomber unknowingly caught in a powerful, nighttime tail wind on its way back to North Africa? The captain and crew made the fatal assumption it just wasn't possible to fly that far that fast. You can imagine how they must have felt when they finally realized they were so far into the Sahara desert they could not possibly get back. Running out of fuel and ditching the plane was inescapable. You can also imagine what went through their minds as they looked around the next morning in the heat of the scorching sun, surrounded by sand as far as the eye could see. All they could do was try to walk out. They died doing so.

The tragedy is that their instruments gave them all the signals they needed to find their way safely home while they still had plenty of fuel to get there. As a society, we are now flying way off course, and fast running out of fuel. The question is, will we change our course and make it back out of danger before we go the way of ancient Greece and the Lady Be Good? The present situation is critical. Like one U.S. senator said, "The evidence is only hidden from the blind."

In 1989, a national commission was formed by the American Medical Association for the purpose of evaluating America's youth. The commission came to the conclusion our youth are in a state of "national emergency," and we are facing an "unprecedented adolescent crisis." They gave their report the title *Code Blue*, which in a hospital signifies a life-threatening emergency, where specialists rush to the bedside of someone whose life is hanging in the balance. The degree of the crisis is evident when you realize that today we have security guards patrolling the halls of many of our public schools. Teachers and students are no longer dealing with spit wads; it's bullets many are concerned about. Who would have thought in the 1950s that we would see the legal killing of 4,000 pre-born children every day in America?

As our society continues its flight into the desert, the instrument panel of our plane is flashing warning lights, and buzzers are sounding all over the cockpit. Actually, the warning lights and buzzers have been flashing and sounding for quite some time. The question is, how have we as a culture dealt with the flashing lights and buzzing sounds? Basically, there are two ways to deal with them. One way is to change direction and get back on the right flight path. The other way is to replace the instrument panel with one which does not flash or buzz when you fly off course.

Regrettably, our society as a whole has made the second choice. Gradually over the past seventy-five years, the instrument panel our great grandparents navigated by has been steadily replaced with a different one – wire by wire, button by button. It hasn't happened in a single day, but over a period of just a few generations, our previously held cultural assumptions have been replaced with new ones. New to us, that is, but not new to history. For these very assumptions are the ones the ancient Greeks used to build their culture upon, only to have it come tumbling down at the feet of the Romans. And like the Trojan Horse, the Romans brought many assumptions from the Greeks into their own Empire, which eventually led to their undoing from within. Now our present culture has done the same, and we are experiencing similar results.

Just what are these Greek assumptions? You will see them clearly as we examine their answers to the following kinds of questions in the chapters to come:

- How did life originate?
- What is "nature"?
- Who, or what, is God?
- What is a human being?
- How do we know what is really true?
- What is morality, and how is it determined?
- What determines the value of children?
- What role should parents play in rearing them?
- What is religion?

- How does religion fit into business and public life?
- What is sacred, and what is secular?
- What is man's purpose in living?

All of these questions, and more, will form the content of this book. So without further introduction, let's begin by taking a look at the matter of origins. It's probably the best place to start, since the answers to so many of the other questions hinge upon how we answer this one.

**CHAPTER ONE SUMMARY: KEY PEOPLE, PLACES AND CONCEPTS**
  The role of assumptions in decisions we make.
  The West as a cultural mixture of Hebrew and Greek assumptions.
  The cultural signs of moral decay.
  The importance of questioning our assumptions.
  The similarities between decadent Greece and the contemporary West.
  The primary contributions of the Greeks to our culture.
  The primary contributions of the Hebrews to our culture.

*For Further Thought and Discussion*

1.  Read through a local newspaper and examine current issues and events by identifying possible unspoken assumptions behind the spoken words or visible acts reported.

2.  "To understand the present, we must understand the past." Explain and justify this statement with examples.

3.  Identify one example of a change of assumption in our culture that we have experienced over the past fifty years. List specific effects this change has had upon our society.

4.  List your personal "life assumptions", and give examples of how these assumptions have practically affected you.

5. If a "Hebraic" perspective emphasizes content first and form second, or essence first and shape second, or character first and credentials second, consider how this way of thinking might affect life in the spheres of education, church, government and parenting.

6. Identify specific assumptions that reflect a "Hebraic" perspective in the above four areas. List behaviors or choices that might occur as a result of these assumptions. For example, a "Hebraic" assumption regarding church might be: "A church is not a building, but a living organism." Some results of such a way of perceiving church might be: in China, when the government shut down church buildings, those who understood the church to be an organism rather than a sanctuary with a specific address, functioned as a church in home "cell groups" throughout the nation.

## Chapter Two

# Who Makes the Snow, God or Mother Nature?

❦

B ill Keane's cartoon, *The Family Circus*, shows little daughter Dolly standing by the living room window looking out at the snow-covered front yard. The caption reads: "I forget. Who gives us snow, God or Mother Nature?"

It's no wonder Dolly is confused. She goes to church on Sunday where she is told God is the Creator of all things, but when she comes home and turns on the T.V. to watch one of those interesting wildlife programs, all she hears mentioned is Nature, with a capital N. Nature with a capital N? Yes. Although we don't often see it capitalized in writing, we often hear it spoken with a capital N. Try tuning in to one of those nature programs yourself and you will hear Its name mentioned frequently. On the screen you see an extraordinary example of a particular animal's behavior, only to hear the voice of the narrator attribute this awesome wonder to the amazing work of 'Nature.' It truly is amazing what Nature has made of Itself!

Maybe you've seen the ad in the travel section of your newspaper that reads like this: "Nature made us the most beautiful islands in the world. Now, so-and-so Hawaiian Holidays is helping make us the most affordable." But, do people today actually believe nature makes itself? Yes, they do. Listen to this definition of nature from the third edition of Merriam-Webster's Unabridged Dictionary: "a creative and controlling agent, force, or principle operating in something and determining wholly or chiefly its constitution, development, and well-being; such a force or agency in the universe acting as a creative guiding intelligence."

This concept of Nature is one in which It clearly is the source of Its own creative power, as though It were some sort of immense perpetual motion machine that just created Itself (intelligently, no less) and keeps going on Its own!

Noah Webster would not be pleased with this definition. We can tell by taking a look at how the original Webster defined nature in his famous dictionary of 1828. This definition dramatically illustrates how much our cultural assumptions about nature have changed since then. Noah Webster tells us nature is, "a word that comprehends all the works of God; the universe." He then quotes Alexander Pope, who tells us to "look through nature up to nature's God." And as though Webster wanted to make sure nobody would possibly misunderstand the meaning of the word nature, he writes these remarkable words:

By the expression, "trees and fossils are produced by nature," we mean, they are formed or produced by certain inherent powers in matter, or we mean that they are produced by God, the Creator, the Author of whatever is made or produced. The opinion that things are produced by inherent powers of matter, independent of a supreme intelligent author, is atheism. But generally men mean by nature, thus used, the Author of created things, or the operation of His power.

If Noah Webster were alive today, he would quickly discover to his astonishment that when most contemporary people use the word nature, they no longer mean "the Author of created things, or the operation of His power." They do indeed mean a self-creating, self-sustaining force that operates "by inherent powers of matter, independent of a supreme intelligent author." In Webster's day, respected leaders made reference to "the laws of nature, and of nature's God." Today, however, we hear about the "laws of nature," while the part about "nature's God" is no longer mentioned. This is because today's prevailing notion of nature has no God under whose laws it functions – Nature is God, functioning by Its own self-created laws, being a law unto itself.

The question of the origin of life, then, becomes simple enough to answer. How did life originate? It made Itself! This grand assumption, so prevalent and commonly accepted today, is not new, by any means. The roots of this idea go back to a specific time and a specific place in history. A time and place you may have guessed by now. Over 2,500 years ago, on the west coast of present day Turkey, there lived a group of ancient Greeks known as the Ionians. It was here that certain unique thoughts about nature took shape, under the guiding hand of a man by the name of Thales. When the Greeks came to name their Seven

Wise Men, they named Thales first. Today he is sometimes referred to as the Father of Western Philosophy. He is credited with the development of what historians call "The Ionian Science of Nature."

The Ionian Science of Nature was a truly remarkable and extraordinary idea. It brought about the beginning of a whole new way of seeing reality. Prior to this time in history, men attributed the activity of nature to various unseen supernatural forces at work behind the scenes. For most of the ancient Greeks, this meant the work of numerous gods atop Mount Olympus, or thousands of nature-spirits of all types and function.

What is so remarkable about the Ionians is, as far as we know, they were the first people in history to dismiss the supernatural altogether. While people around them were paying homage to deities of thunder, sky, and fire, the Ionians started an ancient "gods are dead" movement that never stopped. Here, secular thought was born. As for the Nature-philosophers, like Thales and his follower Anaximander, all that existed was Nature. Period.

Armed with this truly revolutionary concept, Anaximander ventured an explanation for the origin of life. His answer, given nearly 600 years before Christ, went like this: The first living things developed in water. Covered with a hard skin, in time they washed up on the dry banks where they were baked by the sun. After a while the tough outer skin cracked off, and the creatures lived on.

Man's origin, said Anaximander, came about a bit differently. Yes, he too came from the sea, but it would have been impossible for man to have survived if he began like he is now. For man alone has a long period of helpless infancy, and requires a considerable amount of feeding and care before he can fend for himself. No, said Anaximander, "man sprang from a different animal, in fact from a fish, which at first he resembled."[4]

Six hundred years B.C.? You may have thought the theory of evolution was something Charles Darwin thought up in the 19th century. Many people are under this false impression. Of course Darwin developed the theory greatly, and put it in the form of popular books, but the idea that man had previously been in the form of "a different animal" goes back to the ancient Greeks. The most famous ancient Greek scientist of all, Aristotle, who lived about 250 years after Anaximander and 350 years before Christ, believed the ape was an intermediate form of man. This "Father of the Scientific Method," as he is called today, classified man as an animal, and distinguished him from other animals in this way: Man is a rational animal.

Aristotle also believed life forms sprang spontaneously from non-living matter. The question of how this could happen was not a serious problem. The idea of spontaneous generation of organic life from inorganic matter had its roots in ancient religion, going back to the dawn of Greek civilization.

It was held by the earliest ancient Greeks that life forms owed their origin to the earth itself. Mother Earth originally gave birth to every type of plant and animal. Of course this unknowable, impersonal power was not a breathing, thinking, loving mother like the one who birthed you and me, but it did have a life of its own. It was a life generated by itself from within itself. It was a form-less, shapeless, mysterious force, not acting with any human-like reason, but a stream of energy acting randomly upon all things, indifferent to man's desires. Every living thing owed its existence to this creative energy, and none could escape its final pull of death. In the end, it always had its way, drawing each and every life form back down into itself like an inescapable gravity.

This fateful pull of life forms by Earth back down into itself was considered justifiable, because all organic life sustained itself by living off of other living things. This was seen as a great injustice, since the life of one form required the death of another. That expression of pride was eventually avenged by Mother Earth. In Greek, this irresistible pull was called *anagke*, which translated means, "fateful, compulsive necessity."

The mysterious force of Nature fascinated Greek philosopher-scientists like Aristotle, who observed trees being drawn toward light, and concluded it was a power within the material world itself that moved it to behave the way it did. Mother Nature was not at all human, nor was it personal in any way. But it certainly was an active, all-powerful, self-creating and self-sustaining energy. Anaximander referred to it as the "Indefinite-Infinite." Aristotle called it "God." Today, New Age religion uses the same term. Some just call it the "Force", an energy field created by all living things. It surrounds us, and penetrates us. "It binds the galaxy together," as Obi-wan Kenobi described it to Luke Skywalker in Star Wars, one of the most popular American films of the late 1970s.

No matter what name you call it, the idea was absurd to the ancient Hebrew. This book is meant to help us understand why.

## THE EXTRAORDINARY HEBREW GOD

Imagine yourself on a hot summer afternoon, just sitting on the front porch of your home, minding your own business, relaxing in the cool shade of a giant oak tree. You pour some Pepsi over the ice cubes in your glass, and take a long, slow sip. Off in the distance, way down the dusty road, your eye catches three men slowly walking your way, one of whom is the Lord God Himself!

You run out to greet them, inviting them to join you in the shade of your tree. You quickly go to the freezer and grab those T-bone steaks you've been saving for some very special occasion, and insist they stay for a barbecue. And the Lord says, "Love to. Thanks."

A bit out of the ordinary? Of course. Inconceivable? Not really. For this, minus the Pepsi and the freezer, was Abraham's experience one hot desert day while he sat in the door of his tent by the oaks of Mamre. The Lord was on His way to do business with Sodom and Gomorrah (as only He could do it), but en route, He took time to stop by Abraham and Sarah's tent to let them know they would soon have the son He promised long ago, the son necessary for Abraham to become a great and mighty nation, through which all the nations of the earth would be blessed. (You can read all about this unusual visit in Genesis, chapter 18.)

Have you ever stopped to consider just how extraordinary the God of the Bible truly is? Here we have the One who made the galaxies with a word: "Let there be...", and suddenly they appear out of nothing. He tells water, atmosphere, and dry land to take their places on the stage of planet Earth, and then speaks the plants and animals into existence. He makes a man and a woman, and places them in a well-watered garden. And, as though all of this were not astounding enough, He then walks in the garden in the cool of the day, carrying on conversations with the man and woman like a father would with his children.

David wrote in Psalm 86: "Among the gods there is none like you." He had good cause to say it! The God of Abraham, Isaac, and Jacob is totally unique. Compare this God to the Greek gods of Mount Olympus. They were very personal beings for sure. They laughed, they cried. They communicated with men, and made choices by acts of the will. They even bore children. But the gods of Homer were limited in their powers. They did not know all there was to know. They couldn't be every place at once. They were powerless in certain situations.

In fact it was this very man-likeness of the Olympian gods which gave rise to their rejection by Greek philosophers, for they were simply too human to be divine.

Compare the God of Abraham with the Ionian concept of Nature, which is still with us today. While Nature is omnipotent and omnipresent, having no limits to its creative power and presence, it isn't personal. It isn't a being you converse with or know in a personal way. It doesn't love. It doesn't reason. It operates randomly, with no rationale or purpose in mind. By chance it made itself. By chance it made amino acids. By chance they combined to form life. By chance it brought forth a fish – an ape – a man. How much chance is too much chance? How do hidden assumptions improve the believability of chance?

What makes the God of the Hebrew so extraordinary among gods is this: only the God of Israel is entirely personal and unlimited at the same time. There was (and is) no god like Him. He communes with man on a level he can understand, and yet He is the One who created all matter, energy, and time. They do not control Him. He transcends the cosmos, existing independently of nature. He does not subject Himself to the scrutiny of human hands and eyes seeking proof of His existence through observation and measurement, but He reveals Himself to the humble, who seek Him with their whole heart. His existence is not explained. We must come to Him as believing as a child. We are only told He forever has been and forever will be, and He does not change. His position of utter sovereignty is absolute, unqualified, unconditional, and complete. He is Lord over all He has made, and there is nothing in the universe which has come into being apart from His creative act.

Nature is the result of creation, not the cause of creation. God, the personal-unlimited Creator, is distinct from what He has made, and the two are not to be equated or confused. Nature is dependent upon Him for its very existence, and has been subject to His authority right from the start. Nature is not its own master. It did not appear on the scene until God said, "Let there be...", and it will not disappear until He says, "Let there not be..." In the meantime, God holds it all together by His presently active, sustaining power. While the Greeks saw laws of Nature, the Hebrews saw laws over nature.

When we look at creation [a much better word for "nature"], we must not take it all for granted. It isn't "just there," and it doesn't just continue to be there, either. It originally came into being through the premeditated act of God in the first place, and the very fact creation continues to exist today is as much of a wonder as its first appearance. We must not view creation as merely a one-time act of the past, but rather as a continuing deed of the present. It is not as though God made all of creation at some point in the past, and now it functions quite well all on its own. God did not create a cosmic wristwatch way back when, put a self-charging battery in it, and set it off to tick through time complete in and of itself, running according to so-called "natural" laws. Look out your window once again. The present is as magnificent as the beginning, the very continuing existence of the universe as awesome as its first appearance.

In this respect, then, we can say nature itself is unnatural. That is, if it were not for the continuing supernatural action of the creation-sustaining God who keeps on holding it all together, nature would be no more. In terms of how most people think about the natural and the supernatural, the natural has come to mean "the normal operation of a self-governing system," while the supernatural refers to "the interference of God in that system." This concept is unbiblical. Colossians 1:16-17 tells us, "For by Him [Christ] all things were created that are in heaven and that are in earth, visible and invisible, whether thrones or dominions or principalities or powers. All things were created through Him and for Him. And He is before all things, and in Him all things consist [or, hold together]."

No, Dolly, nature does not make the snow. Never has, never will. This is modern mythology in the truest sense of the word. The Bible presents a view in which God the Creator is as active in the continuance of nature as He was in its inception. The elements simply do not function independently of God.

While creation normally functions under ordained laws of physics which God maintains, this does not limit the Lord from choosing at times to supersede His own laws and do things differently. When He does, we call it a "miracle," such as when water was turned to wine, or Lazarus was raised from the dead.

But we must not make the false assumption that God is present in the miracle but stands on the sidelines during the ordinary times. He is equally active and present in both, whether in raising someone from the dead, or raising bread at the local bakery at four a.m. tomorrow morning. The fact that God created matter in the beginning is just as awesome as the fact He is right now holding together the chair on which you sit. He is right now sustaining your very breath. Apart from His continuing choice to hold the very atoms of your body together, you would fall in a heap on the floor and disappear. In fact, you would disappear before you hit the floor. But He sustains you because He wants to know you and to share a relationship with you. Amazing, but true.

The question is, "Who among gods is like unto Him?" The answer is clearly, "No one comes close."

**MADE IN HIS IMAGE**

Take a look at the following assortment of letters and decipher its meaning:

GODISNOWHERE

What did you come up with? If you saw "God is nowhere," you are among the majority. If you saw, "God is now here," you are among the minority. (If you saw both, consider yourself very clever.)

Two different people looking at the very same configuration of letters may see two entirely opposite messages. What's the point? Two different people looking at the very same human being may see two entirely opposite entities. Let's take the human embryo, for starters.

Two highly-trained physicians examine the very same fetus. They both measure it, listen to its heartbeat, and watch it move on the ultrasound machine. One doctor sees the pre-born as an impersonal piece of tissue. Should the mother request, he would just as easily terminate it as he would remove an unwanted lump of cancer, for the price of under $500. The other doctor sees something radically different. And because of what he sees, he would not harm it for any price.

Why this totally opposite response? It is because the conclusions people draw about the nature and value of humans is entirely dependent upon the assumptions they start with regarding how man originated. Think about it for a moment. If that little embryo is really the end result of a long series of chance happenings among impersonal elements of matter, then what would cause it to be anything more than an impersonal assortment of chemicals today? If man had no personal beginning, then there can be no truly personal midpoint somewhere along the way. What began as impersonal amino acid and evolved into a fish is still impersonal chemicals. So is the fish that evolved into man.

The human fetus, then, is still impersonal matter. It has just changed its shape over millions of years. And not only is the embryo just a piece of tissue, but so is the mother who bears it, and so is the doctor! Logically, then, we have no more inherent significance than a dog or a whale. This, no doubt, is what led Oliver Wendell Holmes, former justice of the United States Supreme Court, to say, "I see no reason for attributing to man a significance different in kind from that which belongs to a baboon or to a grain of sand." [5]

If the starting point of human history was the random coming together of amino acids in sea water, then clearly we have no ultimate value or meaning beyond what we may or may not decide for ourselves, as short lived as we may be. This is the only measurement of human value we can possibly have, if we assume we have no ultimate "father" other than the raw elements.

According to Thales, the Ionian, our "father" was water. And today's Ionians aren't far removed from this idea. Occasionally you will read their pronouncements in the newspaper, as on the front page of The Seattle Times, January 27, 1994. Here we are told life originated from microscopic bacteria growing in hot, deep undersea vents, such as those discovered about 200 miles off the coast of Washington State: "'Everything on Earth today evolved from these high-temperature micro-organisms,' [University of Washington] microbiologist John Baross said… 'The beauty of a hydrothermal vent is it works like a chemical reactor,' he said. 'You get every combination of acidity, salinity, temperature and chemicals that you could want' to create life. Eventually one combination might spark the random assembly of amino acids that could lead to self-sustaining life, [Baross] has proposed."

As you can see, the pagan myth of Mother Earth is alive and well today. Now we have found her womb. Such proposals that man is the result of the random assembly of amino acids only serves to dehumanize all of us, at least in the Hebraic sense of the word "human." So what is it, then, which makes a human being "human," according to the Hebraic view? What gives man significant worth? What is the basis of human value, and what is it about our identity that distinguishes us from the rest of matter?

The answers to these questions are found in the remarkable opening chapters of Genesis. Here we see man coming into being not by chance, but by choice. We are the result of a deliberate, premeditated act of the triune God, Who said, "Let us make man…", and so He did! We are created beings by intent.

But the fact that we were created does not set man apart from the rest of creation. The beasts and the beetles were also created, as were the trees and the tides. So what is it that distinguishes us from the other aspects of created reality?

First, we were not created in the same act as the creation of animals. Fish and fowl were created on the fifth day, while man was made on the sixth. Furthermore, the Genesis record tells us that although man was created on the same day as the beasts, he was not created at the same time. After God brought forth the "beasts of the earth... and everything that creeps on the earth," then He said, "Let us make man...".

Second, with regards to man alone, we are told God "breathed into his nostrils the breath of life." We are the only part of creation given this remarkable distinction. But the factors given above still do not provide us with the most significant creation factor of all, namely, man is the only part of creation made in the image of God Himself. Being made in the image of God is the determining factor of our unique identity. This sets man as far apart from the ape as from the ant, or a plant. But what does it mean to be made in the image of God?

To answer this question we must first consider God Himself, whose likeness and image we bear. It is not possible for us to fully comprehend the nature of God. Our limited intelligence can't do it. But it is certainly possible for us to comprehend God to a good degree. We can comprehend the fact our God is highly personal, as we have discussed before. He thinks rational and orderly thoughts. He uses language to communicate meaning and purpose. He makes plans, and follows through by a choice of His will. Furthermore, He has a wide spectrum of emotion, ranging from joy to sorrow, anger to peace, love to hate, and pleasure to disappointment, while never being confused or out of control. He is creative. He is a spiritual being.

In creating man, God made us so that we would resemble Himself in a way other creatures did not. He chose to make man this way because He had a unique and special purpose in mind. This purpose can be summarized in one word: relationship. To have a truly meaningful relationship with man required that we be able to communicate with God on a personal level, on a level with real significance and substance. This required that God create us in His likeness, with shared personal characteristics designed to interact with Himself.

Some modern philosophers, such as David Hume and Immanuel Kant, have led people to believe God is so different from man He could not possibly be known or even communicated with by humans. Some have concluded that human language is simply not adequate for a relationship between the unlimited God and limited man. That is to say, if God were to actually communicate with men through language we could understand, then God would be something less than God.

But the Bible presents God as One who is not only the Creator of the galaxies, being everywhere at once, and knowing all there is to know, but also as fully personal, able to communicate with man through normal words which can be received and understood. The adequacy of human language as a means of communicating God's messages to man, and man's ability to hear and understand these words, is all part of God's creation of man as an image-bearer of Himself. If man were not capable of understanding God through ordinary language, and if His revelation to man could not be expressed in terms of ordinary thought, then man himself would be something less than God created him to be.

With the thought of this kind of relationship in mind, God created man with the ability to think reasonable and orderly thoughts, to create ideas, and to make choices of the will, rather than just function according to preprogrammed instincts, like a bird or a fish. He chose to give man the ability to put his thoughts in the form of spoken and written words, so others could share his ideas, including God, Who enjoyed hearing what Adam had to say. He delighted to bring him the animals and have him name them one by one. He wanted to walk with Adam and Eve through the garden in the cool of the evening, sharing His life with them in the truest sense of the word "share." He loved them, and they loved Him back. This was only possible because God made them with the capacity to love, a capacity they could only have because they were made in His image and likeness. Man is a personal being, because God is a personal being. Man is creative, because God is creative. Man is a spiritual being, because God is a spiritual being.

Of course, God is God and man is man. The two are not the same. While there are certain attributes of God which are mirrored in man, there are other attributes which God alone possesses. No matter how well man thinks and understands, he simply does not understand everything, nor know all there is to know. His capacity to understand is limited by God's design. Likewise, man has been given the capacity to mold and shape the materials of earth into designs of seemingly endless variety, but he simply cannot create something out of nothing. Our creative power is limited. Still, while only God can make a tree, He made only man to prune it. The significance of this must not be underestimated or taken for granted. We are totally unique creations, among all creations on the planet.

The question now becomes, who among the creatures is like unto man? The answer is clearly, none come close. Why? Because we are the only part of creation made in God's image, bearing His likeness. Hebrew, Greek, Asian or African, we are all created in God's image and likeness, by virtue of the Creator's choice, according to the purposes of His design.

Our value as humans, then, must not be based on how others may feel about us, or even on how we may feel about ourselves. It must be based first and last upon the very value of God Himself, whose likeness and image we bear. If God has value, and certainly He does, then you and I have value. If God has worth, then your neighbors have worth, whether they are believers in God or not. Christian or atheist, Hindu or Muslim. God does not love us because we may be Christians. He loved us before we became Christians. "While we were yet sinners, Christ died for us," the Bible tells us. We do not love our neighbors because they are Christians, or even because they may become Christians as a result of our love. We love them because God made them in His image, and because He is precious to us, they who bear His image have value as well.

Apart from everything else, the fact that a person is an image-bearer of God gives each human immeasurable worth. No matter what race or nationality, no matter what abilities we may or may not possess, the indelible stamp of the Creator is on each of us. His image is fixed as surely in the feeble, the lame, the deaf, the dumb, the blind, the poor, and the helpless as it is in the genius. It is the birthright of everyone born of man and woman, who have been bearing "after their kind" since Adam and Eve.

What happens in a culture which fails to recognize this unique basis for human worth? What signs should we be looking for? Once again, we turn to the ancient Greeks for warnings.

## THE VALUE OF HUMAN LIFE IN SPARTA AND ATHENS

A newborn baby's cry broke the early morning air as another human life took breath. A baby boy was born. His deep brown eyes and wavy, coal-black hair bore unmistakable resemblance to his parents. His father and mother were pictures of robust health, and this baby boy seemed healthy, too. Yet, he was considerably smaller than normal, which caused the parents to exchange glances of concern. "We'll let the Council decide," the mother said.

It was the City Council's duty to determine the worthiness of children born into this society. Infants were brought before the Council for official inspection and formal approval. It was for the common good of the city as a whole. The highest standards of strength must be maintained. Even before they brought him to the Council, his parents knew what the outcome would probably be. And they were right. This child was deemed unfit for life.

Removing the baby from his parents (who willingly gave him up), the officials took him to a high cliff and tossed him over the edge. His helpless wail was abruptly cut off by the impact of his tiny body upon the jagged rocks below. A fleeting echo remained but for a moment. Then all was silent once again. This grisly scene really happened. Not once, but many times over. The place was Sparta. The time was about 2,500 years ago. The cliff is on Mt. Taygetus, in southern Greece.

What happens in a culture where the dividing line between man and animal is blurry? The answer is: The two blend into one. People lose their sense of humanity, and act more like animals than men. Such was the case in ancient Sparta.

At seven years of age the Spartan boy was taken from his parents to be brought up by the state. He became part of a military training program which included the most severe forms of discipline. Bearing pain and hardships silently was expected of all. Any signs of cowardice brought days of disgrace. By the age of twelve, they were required to sleep in the open air on a bed of broken rushes from the river bank. Underclothing was not allowed, and only one garment was worn throughout an entire year. They knew no comforts of home, but lived in barracks until the age of thirty. These youngsters were often the homosexual objects of older men.

At the age of thirty a man was admitted to the rights of a citizen and allowed to dine with his elders, where he was required from his thirtieth year to his sixtieth to eat his main daily meal in the public dining hall, the food being deliberately small in amount in order to harden him for war.

As for the girls, they were trained to be strong through running and wrestling. It was a crime not to marry, and husbands were encouraged to lend their wives to other men who were especially strong, so that they would bear children who were also of exceptional strength. It was a form of human selective breeding. We've already seen what happened to the offspring who didn't meet the community standard of strength, and every child was subject to the father's right to infanticide. A king, Archidamus, was even fined for marrying a small wife. As for the character of Spartan women, the Greek historian Plutarch described them as "bold and masculine, over-bearing to their husbands."

What was it that motivated the Spartans to live this way? What assumptions formed the foundation of their city-state? If we search the crawl space of their culture, we find some telling clues in the record left by Plutarch. He described Sparta as a place where "no one was allowed to live after his own fancy; but the city was a sort of camp, in which every man... looked upon himself not so much born to serve his own ends as the interests of his country." [6] He tells us their way of life was fostered by a Spartan lawgiver by the name of Lycurgus, who "bred up his citizens in such a way that they neither would nor could live by themselves; they were to make themselves one with the public good, and, clustering like bees around their commander, be by their zeal and public spirit carried all but out of themselves, and devoted wholly to their country." [7]

As for Lycurgus and his city-state, there was simply no greater good than the good of the group as a whole. In Sparta we find one of the most brazen examples of statism the world has ever known. Statism means the interests of the state provide the sole basis of human worth and moral values. In statism, what is good, moral, honorable, and just is defined in terms of the goals and aspirations of the state itself. Under such conditions, the state sets the standards of value, not only for human lives, but for every human activity. Such values are prescribed by the state, and are relative to the purposes of its self-serving existence.

In Sparta, the will of the state was supreme, and its inhabitants were virtually owned by the city-state from the cradle to the grave. The Spartan army provided the cohesive factor of the culture. To be "good" meant to be strong and brave. The measurement of a man's worth was found in how much he contributed to the strength of the group as a whole. And in the process, the individual was minimized.

In another famous city, about one hundred miles away, we find just the opposite. For in Athens it was the individual whose rights were exalted and upheld. The Athenian statesman Pericles summarized the matter well when he said, "Each single one of our citizens, in all the manifold aspects of life, is able to show himself the rightful lord and owner of his own person, and do this, moreover, with exceptional grace and exceptional versatility."

It was through cultural individualism that the citizens of Athens clarified their values and established meaning for their lives. Their ideals were expressed through the arts, athletics, and education, where they found outlets for complete self-expression. At the heart of it all was personal pleasure and the pursuit of "the good life." J. F. Dobson, of Trinity College, Cambridge, wrote that "the real contrast of principle between the Spartan and Athenian systems is that, while the former, having an eye always to practical matters, considered any kind of culture undesirable, the latter always placed it in the front among the qualifications for a good life." [8]

In Athens, infanticide was commonly practiced, being condoned by both law and public opinion. However, the reasons behind it were much different than in Sparta. Whereas in Sparta it was the elimination of the weak and the small which prompted the killing of infants, in Athens it was the elimination of any child, weak or strong, that threatened the good life. Infanticide was promoted as a safeguard against overpopulation and depletion of natural resources. It was often accomplished by exposing the newborn child to the natural elements in large earthenware vessels, often placed at the temples to their gods. Extreme limitation of the family became one of the outstanding social marks of ancient Greece, with some Greek cities having as few as one family in twelve with two sons, and hardly any having daughters. Eventually the death rate overtook the birth rate.

A child born into an Athenian home was formally accepted into the family sometime within the first ten days after birth. After the child was accepted, he or she was indulged with all kinds of toys: rattles, dolls, clay soldiers, swing sets, spinning tops, kites and marbles. While their Spartan counterparts were being hardened for war, the Athenian kids played hide-and-seek, blindman's bluff and tug-of-war.

From the age of six to eighteen, Athenian boys went to school, where they usually concentrated on literature, music, and gymnastics. Physical beauty, health, and passion were important virtues.

Many different schools of philosophy flourished in Athens, as various teachers expounded their opinions about what truth or virtue really was, and what the proper measure of goodness and meaning should be. It was a philosophic free-for-all, and neither politics, athletics, education, nor the arts could unify Athens into a collective community of mutually applied values. Eventually it fell apart. In 404 B.C., the fleeting Golden Age of Classical Greece came to an end when Sparta defeated Athens in the Peloponnesian War. The soft skin of Athenian scholars was no match for weather-beaten warriors.

Two different cities used two very different standards of measurement for determining human worth and values. One exalted individualism, the other, collectivism. And these concepts – the Athenian exaltation of individualism, and the Spartan exaltation of collectivism – have never died. Both keep repeating themselves on the stage of human history, being played out with different costumes, on different locations, at different times and to different degrees.

But in spite of their seemingly opposite views, we must understand that in essence they both saw life through the very same window. They both shared the same basic, bottom-line assumption, and in this respect both Athens and Sparta were of one mind. It couldn't have been summarized better than it was by one of their own, Protagoras, who declared, "Man is the measure of all things."

Whether measured in terms of the individual man or the collective man, this was their common ground. And this, in seven words, explains why Athens and Jerusalem could not coexist.

**CHAPTER TWO SUMMARY: KEY PEOPLE, PLACES AND CONCEPTS**

Ionia

Thales (c. 640 B.C.)

Anaximander (610-547 B.C.)

Aristotle (384-322 B.C.)

Mount Olympus

The scientific method

The Ionian Science of Nature

Nature (capital N)

The secularization of thought

The Indefinite-Infinite force

Evolution

Spontaneous generation

Naturalism

Unlimited-impersonal force (of Nature)

Personal-limited gods (of Homer)

Personal-unlimited God (of the Bible)

The Olympian gods

Laws of nature versus laws over nature

Sparta

Athens

Being made in the image and likeness of God

Transcendent

Imminent

Statism

Infanticide

The collective will

Mother Earth versus Father God

Anagke

Man is the measure of all things

*For Further Thought and Discussion*

1. When it comes to the matter of origins, why is it impossible for a person to hold to any position other than one of faith? Explain why an atheist is a person of faith as much as is a Christian.

2. If people accept the assumption that human beings are the result of the random activity of chemicals over time, and we are only a part of the self-creating, self- sustaining, impersonal power or force called "nature," then what practical effects might this way of thinking have upon the fields of medicine, civil government, and law?

3. Identify what practical outcomes have occurred as a result of the way of thinking described in question 2 above, and support your thoughts with historical examples or current practice. For example: (In medicine) "To accept this assumption might allow people to justify the harvesting of human organs for profit, prior to natural death. Why not? It would be helpful to the recipient, and besides, some people's lives just don't have that much value to society, you know." (Such organ harvesting has been practiced in recent years.)

4. Compare and contrast the God of the Bible with the god of Nature.

5. Consider ways in which being made in the image of God distinguishes man from animals and truly makes him a unique creation. Discuss how these attributes affect man's position of accountability for his actions.

6. If a person accepts the assumption that all people are "image-bearers of God," how might this affect the way he or she relates to others?

7. After God created everything, He declared it to be good. What is it about creation (including man) which qualifies it to be called "good"?

8. It is significant that man had no vote in the matter of creation and was not consulted prior to construction. What important message does this communicate?

9. Compare and contrast the value system of Athens with that of Sparta.

10. Explain the meaning and significance of this statement: "One must not view creation as merely a one-time act of the past, but rather as a continuing deed of the present."

11. Discuss how creation "speaks," and what it is saying.

12. What is the unifying factor between the so-called "natural" realm and the "supernatural" realm? How are these realms different? How are they alike? Compare and contrast a secularist's definition of the "supernatural" with that of a Christian.

# Chapter Three

# Moral Order and Reason

Here is a simple riddle. What do a carpenter, a cook, and an airplane pilot all have in common? Consider: a carpenter pulls out a level from his tool box and places it along the edge of a 2x4 to make sure it is straight. A cook reaches for a tablespoon and fills it with honey before adding it to her apple pie mix. An airplane pilot watches the instrument panel of his plane while making a landing in heavy fog.

Answer: they all depend upon objective instruments of measurement to do their jobs.

The human senses, as amazing as they are, do have limitations. No matter how well we may think and understand, we simply do not understand everything. We do not know all there is to know, nor are we able to be consistently accurate in our perceptions. Our senses are simply not trustworthy under all circumstances. The example of the airplane pilot is a good case in point.

Imagine you are the pilot of a small, single-engine airplane, making a solo flight over a high mountain range. As you begin your flight the weather is clear and visibility is excellent. But as you approach the high mountains you encounter thick clouds. After entering the whiteness of the clouds and traveling for some distance in zero visibility, you notice some unusual things beginning to happen. Your instrument panel indicates your small plane is banking increasingly to the left, causing you to lose altitude and stray off your necessary course. But your natural sense of balance, as well as the sound of the engine you know so well, tells you differently. Your natural senses tell you that you are not banking at all, and you should continue your flight pattern as is. You assume your instruments must be malfunctioning at this high altitude, and you decide to trust your natural senses rather than follow the seemingly erroneous instruments.

Moments later the truth of the situation becomes painfully evident as you realize with horror that you are headed straight for a solid wall of stone. This illustration is all too true. More than one pilot has lost his life because he did not accept what his instrument panel was telling him, but rather chose to fly according to what he sensed was true. Pilots flying in the fog simply must look to an objective source of trustworthy information to keep from crashing. At times they must deliberately disregard what their mind is pushing them to believe, and lean upon the instrument panel for safety and a successful flight. They must be trained to diligently read the instruments and interpret signals properly.

An uneducated pilot is one who does not understand what the instruments are telling him; a foolish pilot is one who does not watch the instruments when he needs to; a stupid pilot is one who flies in the fog without them. Which is worse? It hardly matters. The results are all the same. At times, the human tendency to think we know better than the objective instruments is stronger than we are willing to admit. Even the most experienced pilots can make a foolish decision. Think back to the Lady Be Good, the World War II bomber that had to be ditched in the Sahara desert. This crew was not stupid, nor were they uneducated. But even the most highly trained can make a foolish fatal choice. And when it comes to fatal choices, all it takes is one. The fact of the matter is, even the best of instruments cannot compensate for human disregard.

Carrying this analogy over to the measurement of human values and morality, we can easily see how different the Hebrew and Greek ways of determining right from wrong really were. For the Hebrew, an objective, superhuman source of information was an absolute necessity in defining human values. This objective source was the Word of the personal-unlimited God of Abraham, Isaac and Jacob. Understanding this superhuman source of information and applying it to their lives was critical to their well-being. That's how Moses, Solomon, and the Apostle Paul saw it. These men, and others like them, believed that to look within themselves, or to look within one's society, for the standards by which to measure values was to look in the wrong direction. Paul warned that those who measure themselves by themselves are unwise. Man was to look outward, to an objective instrument panel for successful flying in life. Not to understand this instrument panel (the Word of God) was to be uneducated, and to disregard it was foolish. And to say "man is the measure of all things" was stupidity, which explains why the study of Greek philosophy was not tolerated in Hebrew schools.

According to the Hebrew model, man is not qualified in and of himself to be his own standard of moral or ethical measurement. The human heart is "deceitful above all things" (Jeremiah 17:9), and certainly cannot be leaned upon as a reliable source of guidance. In fact, often what the human heart would lead man to do is just the opposite of what is right. Like the pilot disoriented in the clouds, there is a way that seems right to a man, but the end result is death. The constant tendency of a person to want to do things his own way must be counteracted by a conscious choice to look to the objective instrument panel and adjust the flight path accordingly.

For the Hebrew, then, it was neither the individual nor the group that could rightly shape human values, mold truth, or measure morality. This was the job of someone objective to man, who stood above the individual and the group, to whom both were equally subject: the Creator/Designer. It was the higher code of the Word of God that provided the objective standard by which all things were to be measured. It was God's unchanging law, which the passing of time could not effect. For the Law of Yahweh was never subjected to vote, public opinion, nor human approval. It was simply nonnegotiable.

Rabbi Immanuel Jakobovits, chief rabbi of the British Commonwealth of Nations, came to the point when he wrote that Judaism "emphatically insists that the norms of moral conduct can be governed neither by the accepted notions of public opinion [the collective group] nor by the individual conscience [the single person]. In the Jewish view, the human conscience is meant to enforce laws, not to make them. Right and wrong, good and evil, are absolute values which transcend the capricious variations of time, place, and environment, just as they defy definition by relation to human intuition or expediency. These values, Judaism teaches, derive their validity from the divine revelation at Mount Sinai, as expounded and developed by sages faithful to, and authorized by, its writ." [9] The Hebrews believed that without God there is no basis for objective ethics.

Note the key words here: "right and wrong, good and evil, absolute values derive their validity from the divine revelation." The very words "absolute values" were foolishness to the Greeks. Values could never be "absolute" in Athens. They could only be relative. Relative to the various viewpoints and opinions of the people who held them. For the Greek, truth was something subjective. That is, it was subject to the opinions of humans who defined it in their own terms, measuring it by standards they set up for themselves. With human reason as their starting point, the philosophers of Athens came up with many different schools of thought about what was true and what was not. This is why, as Doctor Luke noted in the seventeenth chapter of Acts, the philosophers of Athens "spent their time in nothing else but either to tell or to hear some new thing." (NKJ)

The Sophists argued that truth was a matter of individual opinion. Socrates, and later his pupil Plato, sought goodness and truth through the recognition of ideals which lived on even after the people who held them had died. Aristotle sought truth through observation and measurement. Others, such as the Stoics, Epicureans, and Skeptics, tried to define ethics and morality in relation to the happiness of man.

Here, then, is the basic difference between the Hebraic view of truth and the Greek view: the Greeks based their culture upon the assumption that human reason was a sufficient starting point for determining truth, measuring values, and molding morality, while the Hebrews based their culture upon the assumption that divine revelation was the only sufficient starting point for such things.

Yet both positions are equally positions of faith. One position (revelation) rests its faith upon an objective base, and the other position (reason) rests upon a subjective base. To use the analogy of flying again, the pilot who expresses faith in the instrument panel is resting his faith on the reliability of those instruments and acting accordingly. The pilot who expresses faith in his own sense of balance is resting his trust upon the reliability of his mind and senses alone. But neither pilot is taking a step of "blind" faith that could be called irrational or unfounded, for the faith of both is based upon what the person perceives to be an adequate base on which to rest his faith and put his trust. The only problem here is that when one is flying in the fog, the unaided senses are simply not adequate. A step of "blind" faith would be like a pilot in the fog who rests his faith on neither the instrument panel nor his natural senses, but chooses to close his eyes, take his hands off the controls altogether, and just believe everything will turn out all right in the end. This is not faith at all, but pure insanity.

The point here, is that to put one's faith in revelation is not an irrational or unreasonable thing to do. If the Bible really is God's revelation to man, then a person who looks to the Bible for the standard of measurement for morality and truth in his life is not throwing his brains away, or casting all reason aside. He is simply choosing to rest his faith on something outside of himself, in the same way a person who rejects the Bible is choosing to rest his faith on his own sense of what is right and true.

Solomon advised men to trust in the Lord with all their heart, and not to lean on their own understanding (Proverbs 3:5). He learned from his own painful crash how true this was, which goes to show that even the wisest of men are capable of making foolish turns in flight. Moses gave the Hebrews severe warnings about what would happen to their lives and their culture if they neglected to live according to the ground rules provided for them by their Maker. But at the same time, He let them know about the abundant blessings they would experience when they lived in harmony with God's Word. Hebrew faith did not abandon reason. It simply gave it a much different place than the Greeks.

### REASON OR REVELATION?

In June of 1928, an ocean liner called the Tuscania docked in New York City, having sailed across the Atlantic from Europe. On board was a young man by the name of Morris Frank. He was returning from Switzerland, where he had gone to get a dog – a beautiful, female German shepherd by the name of Buddy. Why had he traveled so far for a dog? Because this was a Seeing Eye dog, and Morris Frank was blind. What was so significant about this dog was the fact that Buddy was the first Seeing Eye dog to come to North America. Morris was on a mission to open a training school for guide dogs, called The Seeing Eye.

On the day Morris and Buddy landed in New York, reporters were on hand to catch a story, and Morris was not about to disappoint them. One of the reporters asked Morris if the dog could take him anywhere. Of course Morris said she could. And with that, the reporter said, "How about across West Street?"

West Street, back in 1928, was better known to New Yorkers as Death Street. It was a very broad street along the Hudson River waterfront which crossed a cobblestone area as wide as a football field. There were no traffic lights, and huge trucks, taxis, and draft horses pulling wagons all mingled in a mass of honking, roaring traffic. It was one of the most dangerous streets in the country.

Morris was anxious to let the world know what a Seeing Eye dog could do, so he took the challenge. If he was hurt, however, the whole world would know about it, and The Seeing Eye school would be finished before it started. Morris Frank tells us in his own words what happened:

We entered a street so noisy it was almost like entering a wall of sound. She went about four paces and halted. A deafening roar and a rush of hot air told me a tremendous truck was swooshing past so near that Buddy could have lifted her nose and touched it. She moved forward again into the ear-splitting clangor, stopped, backed up, and started again. I lost all sense of direction and surrendered myself entirely to the dog. I shall never forget the next three minutes. Ten-ton trucks rocketing past, cabs blowing their horns in our ears, drivers shouting at us. One fellow yelled, "You d*** fool, do you want to get killed?" When we finally got to the other side and I realized what a really magnificent job she had done, I leaned over and gave Buddy a great big hug and told her what a good, good girl she was. "She sure is a good girl," exclaimed a voice at my elbow. One of the photographers. "I had to come over in a cab, and some of the fellows who tried to cross with you are still back on the other side!" [10]

Do you suppose Morris Frank's mind was in a neutral, passive state as Buddy led him through that very dangerous situation? Hardly. In order for him to successfully cross that maze of traffic and hostile humanity, his mind had to be fully engaged with the task at hand. It took tremendous concentration on his part to disregard the swirl of moving cars and trucks, the angry shouts of irritated drivers, and the blaring horns. His intellect was not on hold. He put his undivided attention upon the signals which were coming to him up through the harness handle he held with one hand. It took great courage mixed with total trust in that objective source of information known as a Seeing Eye dog, a trustworthy source of input which allowed a blind man to go where even men with 20-20 vision could not follow.

The man who crossed New York City's Death Street with a dog may have been blind, but his faith was not. His faith rested upon something very tangible and reliable, which existed outside of himself, in a well-trained dog named Buddy. No, this was not "blind" faith at all. This was intelligent faith. This was reasonable faith.

Morris Frank could have tried to cross Death Street on his own. It would have been a foolish and unreasonable thing for him to do. Instead, he chose to hold on to the leather harness of a Seeing Eye dog and submit himself entirely to the animal. Under the circumstances, it was the only intelligent and responsible thing for him to do.

All of this, of course, is an analogy: to trust in the Word of God, and to submit oneself fully to it, even when one's heart or intellect wants to lead another way, is not an unreasonable or irrational thing to do. It is the only intelligent thing to do! To ascertain truth through divine revelation, then, is a reasonable and rational use of human intelligence, because we have something trustworthy to lean upon. Revelation is not something which bypasses the human capacity for reason, but rather it is something to which human reason submits, and finds satisfaction and pleasure in so doing.

Once reason thinks it knows better than revelation, and places itself above God's Word, watch out. It is like Morris Frank getting halfway across West Street, then deciding Buddy's signals are not really reliable after all, and choosing to make his own judgment calls about when to proceed and when to stop. Most likely Morris would have become another Death Street statistic.

Human reason was not designed to function independently of divine revelation. It's God's job to provide the signals, and it's our job to read them properly and respond accordingly. To do so is to act responsibly. When it comes to acting irresponsibly, there seems to be no end to the things human reason will justify, given enough time and mental gymnastics to plead its case. As we noted before, our society has flown unbelievably far into the desert over the past forty years. Just compare the content of today's newspaper with that of 50 years ago and you will readily get the message. The following is just one example of something you would not have read in the newspaper in the 1950s. It appeared in the Sunday edition of *The Seattle Times*, on March 20, 1994:

Dr. Georgia Witkin, author, nationally known speaker, and assistant professor of psychiatry and of reproductive sciences at Mount Sinai School of Medicine in New York City, states that sexual "affairs for the widowed and divorced in later years are *not* foolish. [Emphasis by Dr. Witkin.] In fact, they may be healthy for you." She goes on to justify her statements with the following reasons: "[They can] provide enough activity for a mild workout, stimulate enough cortisol to ease the discomfort of arthritis and allergies, and help prevent migraines. Psychologically, a sexual relationship can help prevent depression, increase self-esteem, encourage weight control and counteract stress."

Here you have human reason in full bloom. Revelation has no place in Dr. Witkin's advice, in spite of the fact her school is called Mount Sinai. However, since God clarified the matter many years ago at the original Mount Sinai, we can say it is both responsible and intelligent to abstain from physical intimacy outside of marriage, no matter what your age.

Many other examples could be given, but the important thing to understand here is that when it comes to deciding how we should do business, how we should parent, how we should work, what kind of person we should marry, etc., the basic question we must ask ourselves is: are human minds and senses sufficiently equipped and qualified in and of themselves to be the final judges of what is right, proper, good, and true, or does one need assistance from a super-human source beyond man's limited experience and reason?

The Hebrew position is one that acknowledges the need for objective, superhuman assistance, because the unaided mind of man has limitations, and is simply not sufficiently equipped to ascertain the full picture independently. The Greeks, on the other hand, had no objective source or standards of moral measurement to which all men were equally obligated to submit. They had no Bible, no Word of God. This makes sense when you realize they did not believe in a personal and unlimited God. The common masses of people believed in many limited gods, and the philosopher-scientists believed in no god, except impersonal Nature, and It didn't speak a word, of course.

Objective revelation and the moral absolutes that come with it were clearly not a part of the Greek mindset, nor were they essential to their way of life. Moral and civil law, family life, business, and interpersonal relationships were regulated by standards put in place by man, measuring himself by himself, whether individually or collectively. As a result, there were many different ideas about how to live, and many different expressions of values, often conflicting with one another. Because theirs was a "worship the god of your choice and live by the creed of your need" society, Greek religion and philosophy served to divide Greece as much as unite it. Each man could decide for himself which gods he would worship. There were thousands to choose from. Every part of earth and sky was personified as a deity. And those who rejected the gods had plenty of philosophies from which to choose.

Of course, the Hebrews were free to use their reasoning abilities when making decisions and determining direction for their lives, but it was understood that they were obligated to stay within the borders provided by God's Word.

It is not a question of whether or not human reason is something "bad." On the contrary, reasoning power, in and of itself, is a very good thing. It is a reflection of God's likeness in man. But the fact remains, just as man has limits to his physical attributes, he also has limits to his mental attributes and reasoning ability. A wise man (and a wise culture), will recognize these limits and not try to function beyond them.

For many people today, just as in ancient Athens, such thinking is considered anything but intelligent, and to speak of "borders provided by God's Word" is repulsive. It means that morality is something imposed upon us, and this is "politically incorrect," even if it is God who does the "imposing." After all, to speak of borders and restrictions is contrary to the whole concept of freedom, is it not? Well, let's reason together about this for a moment or two.

### WHAT IS FREEDOM?

After twenty years behind bars, an inmate is finally released from prison. As he walks out the open door, he is heard to say, "At last, I'm free as a bird!"

Freedom is a slippery concept. It's hard to pin down exactly what it means sometimes. In the name of freedom one man gives his life in battle, while another man refuses to fight. In America, the "land of the free," where independence is celebrated every year as a national holiday, cries for freedom have been ringing out for over three hundred fifty years. At first there was a cry for freedom to worship, but in recent years we've heard a much different sound. In the 60s "free love" became a license for immorality, and in the 80s "free choice" became an excuse for abortion.

To many people, the word freedom brings to mind thoughts of doing whatever we want, whenever we want. It connotes being under no obligation, of speaking one's own mind and making one's own choices without interference from others. To be free conjures the image of a man who, like Pericles of Athens described, is "able to show himself the rightful lord and owner of his own person."

But is this what Jesus had in mind when He said, "You shall know the truth, and the truth shall make you free"? Did He mean we would be able to show ourselves to be the "rightful lord and owner of our own person"? If He didn't have this in mind, exactly what did He mean by "free"?

Let's go back to the image of the inmate walking out of prison, saying to himself, "At last, I'm free as a bird!" Think for a moment, not about the man, but about the bird. Let's say the bird is an eagle. Perhaps there is no more dramatic picture of freedom in the entire animal kingdom. In 1776, the Continental Congress chose the eagle to be on the Great Seal of the United States for good reason. The eagle can soar to an altitude of one-half mile, spot a small rabbit from that height (a man would need high-powered binoculars to do this), and then fold its wings and dive for the prey at speeds of 200 miles per hour! But in spite of its splendor, its ability to soar, its incredible eyesight, and capability to hunt, there are definite limits to an eagle's freedom. There are no eagles in the stratosphere, and they do not build their nests under the sea. The eagle has a specific biosphere within which it is free to be an eagle, free to do what an eagle does, free to fly, free to catch small animals, free to build a nest on the side of a cliff, but not free to go beyond the boundaries God set in place. The mighty eagle, our national symbol of freedom and strength, lives within bounds. And so do we.

First, we live within physical bounds. As much as we might like to be Peter Pan at times, we simply cannot soar through the air at will. A man who steps off the edge of a tall building, no matter who he is, will fall to the ground. The law of gravity is no respecter of persons. What it does for one, it does for all. No man is "free" to choose whether or not the law of gravity will act upon him. Yes, he may exercise his free will by jumping off the building, but he is not free to choose the consequences. He has no choice but to fall to the ground, no matter how earnestly he may want it otherwise. The consequences of his action are beyond his freedom of choice.

Second, just like the eagle, we live within mental bounds. As we've said before, no matter how smart a person may be, man's intelligence is limited. We cannot know all there is to know. We cannot see into the future. A "free thinker" can only think so freely.

Third, just as God put in place certain physical and mental limits to our freedom, He also set boundaries to our moral freedom. Here is where man's uniqueness separates him entirely from the eagle. Whereas the eagle lives by instinct in an amoral world without right or wrong, man lives in a moral dimension where issues of good and evil, right and wrong, are daily realities. Moral choices are continually before us. The question is, does man have the freedom to determine his own moral boundaries, or are they already set in place, like gravity?

Here is where Hebrew assumptions collided with Greek assumptions like freight trains in the night. It was the Hebraic position that man has limits to his freedom of choice in the moral dimension just as he has limits in the physical and mental dimensions. It was the Hebraic view that man does not have a free choice to determine his own moral code. He is no more free to decide what ethics applies to him than he is free to decide what laws of physics apply. Yes, he may choose to violate the moral code God put in place, just as he can choose to jump off the edge of a tall building, but in either case, the consequences are such that to boast of "freedom of choice" is grossly misleading.

For man, the moral code is not a matter of choice. When God gave Moses the Ten Commandments, He did not present them as the "Ten Suggestions," or the "Ten Options." He did not tell Moses the people were free to choose His commandments or to design alternatives of their own. This moral code was determined by God for man. Moral law is transcendent law. That is, it exists above and independent of man, just like the law of gravity and every other created law of order. Man does not invent these laws, he recognizes them, accepts them, and lives at peace with them.

Although man possesses the power to act contrary to these laws, this does not mean he has the authorization to do so. While Cain possessed the power to murder his brother Abel, his measure of freedom did not include the freedom to decide for himself whether his action was right or wrong, nor the freedom to determine his own consequences. One might say man has "freedom" to violate the moral code in the same way he has "freedom" to jump off the edge of a tall building, if you want to call that freedom. Yes, if a man chooses to jump off the edge, God is not going to stop him. But neither is He going to stop the law of gravity from acting upon him, and if he has no choice but to fall to the ground, he is not free at all. "Free love"? "Free choice"? A man must consider the consequences before he leaps. Man is not free to break God's moral laws. God's laws, when violated, break men. And cultures, too.

Although the ancient Greeks were very religious in the sense they worshiped many gods and paid homage to hosts of spirits, Greek religion simply did not provide a standard basis for morality common to all men. Their religion did not speak in terms of what was absolutely right or wrong, good or evil for everyone. What was "good" or "bad," "true" or "false," was relative to the individual or group who defined its terms. For apart from the recognition of a transcendent moral code to live by, man is on his own to determine his alternatives, deciding for himself what ought or ought not to be, acting as "the rightful lord and owner of his own person." Morality, then, becomes a relative matter. Relative to the individual, the group, the time, or the circumstance. This, in essence, is the meaning of moral relativism, which some have confused with moral freedom.

In a culture which embraces moral relativism, it doesn't take long before the dividing line between good and evil, right and wrong, becomes meaningless. After all, who is to say what is really good or bad, right or wrong, in a world without an objective standard of "rightness/wrongness" by which all opinions must be measured? In a society of moral relativism, one man's opinion is as good as another. While for the Greek, truth was often a matter of opinion, for the Hebrew, opinion had little to do with truth. After all, when God had spoken, who was man to argue back?

With this understanding of transcendent, God-given laws of physics and morality must come the realization that man was created to fit harmoniously into a world which was ordered by someone other than himself. It was a matter of God's free choice, not our own. It was His idea, not ours.

Being on the receiving end of creation means man can only take things the way they come. That is, he breathes air because this is the way his lungs were made to function. He walks on two legs because this is the way God designed him to walk. Man did not vote on the matter, nor was he consulted prior to construction. God is God the Creator, and man is man the created. We must keep the original order straight.

The reality of our position as created beings living in a world functioning under the transcendent laws of the Creator is something we must simply accept for what it is: the rightful expression of His Lordship and ownership over all. Man can never be the ultimate center of life. God is. He alone is the Lord and rightful Owner of everything. This is the truth, and the sooner we know it, the sooner we are truly free.

What, then, is freedom? Freedom, in a world of transcendent law and orderliness, is the recognition of those laws and living in harmony with them. To be free, then, means to submit oneself to the prescribed order of things, and function responsibly and creatively within the boundaries God has lovingly provided for our good and well-being. Genuine freedom is the internal self-control that comes from self-government under God, through the enabling of the Holy Spirit, regardless of the circumstances.

The Bible does not hesitate to tell men what they may or may not do, because the God of the Bible is intent on the highest good of man. His commands are an expression of responsible love for mankind, like the love of a parent who warns a child to keep his hands away from a hot stove. God's laws are consistent with His love. Those who understand God's laws to be something good embrace them with joy. They do not resist them or see them as "impositions." They seek them out. They delight in the order of the Lord and they become like a "tree firmly planted by streams of water, which yields its fruit in its season, and its leaf does not wither; and in whatever he does, he prospers," (Psalm 1:2-3).

Jesus said "keep My commandments" in the same breath as "these things I have spoken to you, that my joy may be in you, and that your joy may be made full," (John 15:10-11). The Apostle Paul called himself a "bond slave" of the Lord and a "free man" in Christ. Here, then, is one of the great paradoxes of life: human freedom is found in submission to the will of God. What sounds like bondage to the Greek is in reality the ultimate freedom, and what sounds like freedom to the Greek is the ultimate human bondage.

### WHO RULES PLANET EARTH?

Who rules planet earth? Ask many Christians and they will tell you, "God does!" Others will say, "The devil!" But, strangely enough, back in the beginning, God Himself had this to say: "Let Us make man in Our image, according to Our likeness; and let them rule over the fish of the sea and over the birds of the sky and over the cattle and over all the earth, and over every creeping thing that creeps on the earth," (Genesis 1:26). God tossed the ball into our court, right from the start of the game. These are His first recorded words of purpose regarding mankind, proclaimed before Adam was made. But before we go too far in our wild imaginations, we must stop and get the picture into focus, in the proper context. While He did give us a charge to rule over all the earth, He did not give us a license to rule it any way we please. In an ultimate sense, God certainly is the Ruler over all. And, as we pointed out earlier in this chapter, there are basic ground rules we are expected to follow. If we think we can play the game by our own set of rules, we are gravely mistaken.

Yet, instead of focusing on what we cannot do in our limitations, let's focus on what we can do in our freedom. For within the borders of our human boundaries, God has given us an astounding freedom, and the highest place of honor among all living things. David, the Hebrew shepherd-king, pondered this while out under the stars at night: "When I consider Your heavens, the work of Your fingers, the moon and the stars, which You have ordained, what is man that You are mindful of him, and the son of man that You visit him? For You have made him a little lower than the angels and You have crowned him with glory and honor. You have made him to have dominion over the works of Your hands; You have put all things under his feet," (Psalm 8:3-6, NKJ).

Man was commissioned to manage God's very creation! That which He spoke into existence and proclaimed to be good, He entrusted into the hands of human beings for care and stewardship. Man, being created in God's image, was thoroughly equipped for the task because the capacity for rulership is also one of the central aspects of what it means to be made in the likeness of God. Even as God is the infinite Governor of the universe, He made a likeness of Himself to be a finite governor on earth. We are the only creatures given stewardship over all the earth. It is a mandate of utmost responsibility, and a position of tremendous honor.

At the same time, we must realize that even though we have been commissioned to rule over planet Earth, we have not been given ownership of it. It is not our world, it belongs to Another: "The earth is the Lord's, and all it contains, the world and those who dwell therein," (Psalm 24:1). Furthermore, man was not crowned King, he was only made a deputy. Our rulership is like that of a viceroy, governing over a territory or province as the representative of a sovereign or king, accountable to this higher authority, having delegated powers and authorization. Yet, in our case, delegated by God Himself.

Therefore, man's commissioned position of glory and honor as the crown of creation, ruling over all God made in the earth, carries with it certain accompanying obligations. For as with any appointed role of delegated authority, man is in a position of accountability to the One who gave him that authority in the first place. Anything less than this would be license for anarchy on the earth, with each man doing what is right in his own eyes, which (as always) leads to problems.

The Bible is repeatedly clear on this matter: There is only one Lord, and it is not you or me. As for why He chose to govern earth through the delegated authority invested in man, the Scripture does not make clear. Considering how we've managed to make such a mess of things, it's a wonder we've still got the job. The fact remains, however, we were created to rule, and to rule with dignity under God.

Unlike the monkey, man could not be programmed by instinct to behave in predicted ways. Being made in the likeness of God would not allow it, and being equipped for responsible stewardship over the earth requires much more than animalistic instincts. It requires the workings of a decision-making will with a very high degree of freedom. It requires the will to rule responsibly, the will to create, the will to mold and develop, and the will to care. To be controlled by instinct would have meant man was something far less than God intended him to be. God was not out to make more animals. He made a person who would have the capacity to rule with initiative, creativity, and pleasure.

With regards to man's earthly rulership, we should point out that just as God grants to each of us varying abilities and varieties of gifts, He does not intend for every person to be the president of their nation. When we think of rulership, do not think of it simply in political terms. Rulership is something expressed by people of all ages, in every setting imaginable, in ways uncountable, often in the form of responsible stewardship. For a child, rulership may take place in the context of keeping a bedroom clean, and caring for a pet dog. As we grow older, our sphere of stewardship widens. For adults, rulership may take place in the home as well as the marketplace, whether expressing dominion over one's front yard, garden, or kitchen, or ruling over various spheres of responsibility at the office, or in a factory, such as using a word processor, or riveting an airplane wing together.

Everyone, with the exception of the very youngest of children, has some aspect of creation over which responsible stewardship may be exercised. For some, it may be a relatively little "pea patch" of life, while for others, it may be an entire nation.

Now, pause and think for a moment. Consider your own sphere of responsibility. What has He placed into your hands? What has He given you to steward? To care for? To cultivate? To dress and keep? What has He put before you to develop? To foster? To invent? To refine? To advance? In what ways are you using those endowments He gave you in the likeness of Himself to care for and cultivate His world?

### FOUR MISCONCEPTIONS ABOUT THE FALL OF MAN

"Of every tree of the garden you may freely eat; but of the tree of the knowledge of good and evil you shall not eat, for in the day that you eat of it you shall surely die," (Genesis 2:16-17, NKJ).

With the command not to eat of a particular tree, man was confronted with the reality that someone else was in a place of higher authority. The matter of transcendent law was established right here, and has never left us. Up until the third chapter of Genesis, Adam and Eve enjoyed total harmony with God. Things were as they should be, in order and beautiful. Man had never experienced disorder, or "wrongness." But with the first act of disobedience they suddenly understood the difference between good and evil, because the reality of wrongness became their own personal experience. Suddenly they knew what guilt was all about. And with guilt came shame, fear, blame, and pain. Buried behind a barrier of broken fellowship with God, Adam the innocent died that day.

By the fourth chapter of Genesis, Cain murders his brother Abel in jealous anger and then denies his deed before God. By the time we reach chapter 6, the corruption of mankind is so great that the Lord Himself is sorry He made man, and "He was grieved in His heart," (Genesis 6:6). What separates chapter 2 from chapter 4 and all that follows, is the most catastrophic event in the history of man: the Fall.

The Fall was a frightful turning point in history, not only for Adam, but for all his descendants. As a result of the first sin, Adam and all who were "in his loins," became something other than what God originally made them to be. Through Adam's act of willful disobedience, the original image of God became marred, misshapen, and distorted. At the Fall, man became something God was not – a breaker of moral law. He had willfully chosen to "jump off the edge of a tall building," and the consequences were unavoidable for all of us. Man now stood in need of restoration. Not only Adam, the first individual man, but every ongoing extension of himself, linked through time by his offspring, born after his kind, bearing the likeness and image of himself (Gen. 5:3) needs restoration.

Although there is a great deal of mystery about the Fall and exactly what happened inside man on the day that he "died," there are some common misconceptions surrounding the Fall which have led to some unfortunate conclusions over the years. Rather than focus here on what the Fall means for mankind, let's focus on what the Fall does not mean.

1. *The Fall does not mean God forfeited His creation, or His position as Lord over all.*

The world and all it contains are as much God's after the Fall as before the Fall. He made it, He continually holds it together, and He owns it all. The Fall did not change that. In Psalm 50:10-12 God says, "For every beast of the forest is Mine, the cattle on a thousand hills. I know every bird of the mountains, and everything that moves in the field is Mine. If I were hungry, I would not tell you; for the world is Mine, and all it contains." (NASB)

Dr. Albert Greene said it well, "There is a subtle derailment which often occurs in Christian thought at the point of the Fall. We tend to think that when man sinned, God simply relinquished the whole creation as a botched job and left Satan to do what he wanted with it. Nothing could be further from the truth." [11]

Even after the Fall, the earth and all it contains remains His. This is what makes the Fall such a tragic thing. It is His creation that is fallen, and remains His in its fallen state. It is important to understand that the earth and all it contains does not belong to Satan: "The earth is the Lord's, and all it contains, the world and those who dwell in it," (Psalm 24:1). Although the devil may act like he owns the earth and a lot of people who live in it, he simply does not.

The truth of God's ownership and continuing Lordship over all the earth remains true in spite of man's choice to act contrary to His authority, or disregard His rights to our lives. Even though the creature may say to the Creator, "I choose to ignore You and go my own way," it does not alter the fact the Creator is still the King. He is Lord of all, whether a man acknowledges Him as such or not. This has never changed. Of course, it is up to us to recognize Him as Lord, and accept Him as such. It is up to us to receive His forgiveness of sin, and be restored once again into fellowship with Him. But the fact that He is Lord of heaven and earth remains a fact, whether we bow the knee to Him or not.

2. *The Fall does not mean God's intention for man to rule over all the earth was revoked.*

The consequences of the Fall have certainly made the working out of our call to rule over planet Earth much more difficult, but God's command to "be fruitful and multiply, and fill the earth, and subdue it; and rule…", has never been taken back. When one stops to consider the unspeakable things man has done in his role as ruler and steward of the earth, it's a wonder God didn't revoke man's "badge" at the eviction from Eden. But here again, God's provision for redemption through the sacrificial death of Christ allows man to enter into his role of rulership in harmony with God. This was God's original intention for man, and the Fall did not alter His plan.

3. *The Fall does not mean man no longer bears the likeness and image of God.*

Here too is a "subtle derailment" in Christian thought. We tend to think that because man fell, he no longer bears the image and likeness of God. There can be no doubt that Adam and Eve were different after the Fall. They behaved differently, thought differently and had a different heart – a heart that had experienced sin in acting contrary to God. They were separated from God in a way they had not experienced before, and their offspring were born in this separated state. Things were definitely not as they should be, as they were in the beginning. Of course, through sin, certain aspects of the likeness of God were indeed forfeited. Namely, fallen man has a fallen nature, while God certainly does not. In terms of character and moral purity, fallen man is very much unlike God, and falls far short of His likeness. But in spite of man's altered condition, he still bears the image of God as the unique mark of His special creation among all living things. God's gifts of endowments in the likeness of Himself were still necessary for man to fulfill his intended role in the earth and to be able to commune with God on a meaningful level, beyond that of an instinct-governed animal.

It is significant to note in Genesis 9, after Noah and his family went through the flood, God specifically told Noah, "Whoever sheds man's blood, by man his blood shall be shed, for in the image of God He made man," (Gen. 9:6). Here God reaffirms man's image-bearing distinction, after the Fall, and once again declares man's unique and special value among all living things. And this leads us to a fourth important point:

4. *The Fall does not mean man lost his innate value or worth.*

Damaged as he was by the Fall, man continued to have immeasurable value and innate worth. We must not conclude that because man sinned, God discarded him like a broken tool, or considered him worthless. The fact that man continued to have great value and worth in the sight of God even in his fallen state is evidenced by the fact that Jesus went to the ultimate length, death on a Roman cross, to redeem fallen man and restore him. This is what salvation is all about. It is God's intent not only to forgive sin, and allow access to fellowship with Himself, but to restore man as one being fully renewed after the image of his Creator (See Colossians 3:9-10; 2 Corinthians 3:18; Ephesians 4:24; Romans 8:28-29).

As mentioned previously, we do ourselves and our neighbors a disservice if we do not recognize the innate value and worth of human beings, Christian or not, as image-bearers of God, even in the fallen state. This failure to recognize man's innate worth has led to a great deal of human misery. It is particularly tragic when we consider the effects this failure has had upon children, to whom we turn our attention next, as we consider the striking contrasts between Greek and Hebrew assumptions regarding children, and how those assumptions have led to much different actions and attitudes toward the little ones.

CHAPTER THREE SUMMARY: KEY PEOPLE, PLACES AND CONCEPTS
    Reason contrasted with revelation
    Reason-based faith; revelation-based faith; blind faith
    Objective versus subjective basis for faith
    Genesis 1:26-28 (the "cultural/dominion mandate")
    Moral law and the meaning of right and wrong
    The Fall (what it is and what it is not)
    The biblical versus the Greek concept of freedom
    Absolute truth
    Autonomous
    Moral relativism

*For Further Thought and Discussion*

1. In what ways is reason compatible with revelation? How is it incompatible?

2. Why is the term "plumb line" a good way to describe the function of God's Word in our lives both individually and collectively? What effects does the lack of a unified plumb line of values have upon any given culture or group of people? If a society does not accept the Bible as its plumb line, what alternatives might it choose to promote and preserve unity? Think of historic examples both past and present.

3. Give a recent example of a "reason-based" idea or act which you have heard, read, or seen in the media. Can you give an example of a "revelation-based" idea or act which you have heard or seen via the media? (Note: "Revelation based" ideas or actions do not have to be consciously identified as such by those who think or do them. Some people may have a Bible-based code of ethics even though they do not know where it came from.)

4. In what ways is "management" distinguished from "ownership"?

5. Why was it not possible for man to have been preprogrammed to live by instinct and yet still fulfill God's purposes for him?

6. If everyone were to truly accept the assumption that man is living under a transcendent and prescriptive moral code, that is, a moral code which is prescribed by God and one that man has no control or power to alter, and is obligated to obey, then many of our current understandings of popular terms and phrases would take on a radically different flavor. Imagine you have been given the task of writing a dictionary to be called The New Christian Dictionary of the English Language, to include the following terms. Write definitions from a biblical frame of reference.

free enterprise:


free love:


free will:


free society:


free choice:


human rights:


For example: In The American Heritage Dictionary, "free enterprise" is defined as: "The freedom of private business to operate competitively with minimal government regulation." This term defined in The New Christian Dictionary might be: "The freedom of private business to operate competitively within the moral and ethical guidelines provided by God in His Word."

# Chapter Four

# Greek Assumptions and Unwanted Children

*❧❦❧*

There was a formula created and used by a group of doctors to determine whether certain babies should live or die. It was called the "Quality of Life" formula. QL = NE x (H + S). According to the formula, a child's Quality of Life [QL] was equal to his or her Natural Endowment [NE] multiplied by the sum of the contribution of the child's Home [H] and Society [S]. Based on the application of this formula to certain newborn babies, it was decided that those not having a sufficient Quality of Life factor would not be given vigorous treatment for infection or acute illness. In other words, the doctors would not try to save their lives, but would allow the children to die.

Is this a true story, or part of a futuristic novel? If it did happen, when and where did it take place? Was it Nazi Germany of the 1940s? Communist Russia of the 1920s? Ancient Athens of 350 B.C.? In fact, it took place in Oklahoma City, mid-America, at the state-run Oklahoma Children's Memorial Hospital. It was part of the hospital's "selective treatment" program, where between 1977 and 1982, it was determined that 24 out of 69 babies born with spina bifida were better off dead than alive. All 24 died; eight others were given treatment at the requests of their parents, even though doctors advised against it. Of these eight, six lived. (You can read all about it in the October 1983 issue of Pediatrics, Vol. 72, No. 4, pp. 450-458.)

This kind of "quality of life" thinking, which leads to the elimination of children, has been around for a very long time. Historically, it is a part of our Western heritage. As mentioned before, infanticide was commonly accepted and widely practiced in ancient Greece. The Spartans tossed unwanted children from the side of Mt. Taygetus, and the Athenians exposed them to the elements in earthen jars placed next to the temples of their gods. It was in line with the thinking of such philosophers as Plato, who advocated that "inferior" children of the ruling class be discarded in the best interests of Athens.[12]

In ancient Greece, the value of children was based upon their worth as perceived by the particular community into which they were born. If a child was viewed as a detriment to the "good life" of Athens, it was eliminated. Or if the child was seen as a hindrance to the strength of the city-state of Sparta, its life was terminated. While in Athens, infanticide was justified on the basis of concern for overpopulation and depletion of land resources, Spartan child-killing of the weak was justified on the basis of upholding a standard of military might. In both Sparta and Athens, the value of a child's life was measured in terms of social benefit, or social detriment – an idea which was revived in the twentieth-century West.

It may be shocking to think of the harshness of Spartans toward weak children. Furthermore, the fact that the children allowed to live were given over entirely to the state at the age of seven may seem just as amazing. But we would be shortsighted if we failed to see that something very similar took place in civilized Germany of the 1930s and 1940s. Adolf Hitler, the modern Lycurgus of his day, claimed, "It is thus necessary that the individual should slowly come to realize that his own ego is unimportant compared with the existence of the whole people, that therefore the position of the single ego is exclusively determined by the interests of the people as a whole."[13]

In Nazi Germany, as in Sparta, the individual's value was only relative to the group – the state. The interests of the state determined human worth. While in Sparta it was the interests of Lycurgus, in the case of Nazi Germany it was the interests of Adolf Hitler. William Shirer in The Rise and Fall of the Third Reich describes the training of German youth for the New Order:

From the age of six to eighteen, when conscription for the Labor Service and the Army began, girls as well as boys were organized in the various cadres of the Hitler Youth. Parents found guilty of trying to keep their children from joining the organization were subject to heavy prison sentences. Each youngster was given a performance book in which would be recorded his progress through the entire Nazi youth movement, including his ideological growth. At ten, after passing suitable tests in athletics, camping, and Nazified history, he graduated into the Jungvolk ("Young Folk"), where he took the following oath: "In the presence of this blood banner, which represents our Fuhrer, I swear to devote all my energies and my strength to the savior of our country, Adolf Hitler. I am willing and ready to give up my life for him, so help me God." [14]

The outcome of establishing the goals and values of Adolf Hitler as the standard for everyone else meant the lives of many individual Germans were indeed given up for him, though for many it was out of no choice of their own. Those who were viewed as an obstruction to the goals of the Reich were disposed of. These not only included Jews, but many Christian leaders as well as weak and handicapped persons of all backgrounds.

During the early to mid-1940s, there was a special agency set up for the purpose of child termination. It was made up of psychiatric and pediatric experts, whose function it was to decide – entirely on their own – which children were to be eliminated. Dr. Fredric Wertham described the working of this agency in his book, *A Sign for Cain*:

The children slated for death were sent to special "children's divisions."… They were killed mostly by increasing doses of Luminal or other drugs either spoon-fed as medicine or mixed with their food. The dying lasted for days, sometimes weeks. In actual practice, the indications for killing eventually became wider and wider. Included were children who had "badly modeled ears," who were bed-wetters, or who were perfectly healthy but designated as "difficult to educate." The children coming under the authority of the Reich Commission were originally mostly infants. The age was then increased from three years to seventeen years. Later, in 1944 and 1945, the work of the commission also included adults. [15]

If we think such kinds of things could never happen in America, we do not fully realize how far our cultural plane has flown into the desert, and how low our moral fuel supply really is. As a matter of fact, we may have already ditched the plane. Even as far back as 1982, legal infanticide hit the headlines when the Indiana Supreme Court officially sanctioned the deliberate withholding of medical treatment and the subsequent starvation of a newborn child known to millions as "Infant Doe." Born with Down's Syndrome, the baby suffered from a blocked esophagus that could have been easily corrected through routine surgery. But the court granted the parents authority to withhold food. After six days, Infant Doe starved to death, not in an earthen jar, but in a modern, sterile American hospital.

You many think we are a long way from killing children with "badly modeled ears." But if you think this, you are dead wrong. Since 1973, Americans have been legally killing thousands of children with "badly modeled ears," and millions more with perfectly shaped ones. The children are just not allowed to live long enough for us to see what their ears look like. They are being killed in the womb before they see the light of day.

How has this happened in such a short time? Wasn't it just in the 50s that legalized abortion and infanticide were unthinkable? That's exactly right, and herein lies an explanation for why it has happened. It all has to do with thinking. What was once unthinkable, became acceptable thought. And what is accepted thought, sooner or later is acted out. Our assumptions have changed. What most Americans assumed years ago to be true about ourselves and our offspring, many no longer hold to be true. There has been a large scale shift of assumptions about who we are and what determines our values. At the present time in our history, many Americans have assimilated those same assumptions held by the ancient Greeks that allowed a few Nazi Germans to justify the elimination of bed-wetters. These very same assumptions are now allowing a multitude of apple-pie-eating Americans to eliminate 4,000 pre-born children a day, before they have an opportunity to sleep in a bed, let alone wet one.

Exactly what change of assumptions are we talking about? Few have put the matter more bluntly in print than Peter Singer, a biomedical ethicist whose commentary appeared in the July 1983 issue of *Pediatrics* (72:128-129):

Whatever the future holds, it is likely to prove impossible to restore in full the sanctity-of-life view. The philosophical foundations of this view have been knocked asunder. We can no longer base our ethics on the idea that human beings are a special form of creation, made in the image of God, singled out from all other animals, and alone possessing an immortal soul. Our better understanding of our own nature has bridged the gulf that was once thought to lie between ourselves and other species, so why should we believe that the mere fact that a being is a member of the species Homo sapiens endows its life with some unique, almost infinite, value?

Once the religious mumbo-jumbo surrounding the term "human" has been stripped away, we may continue to see normal members of our species as possessing greater capacities of rationality, self-consciousness, communication, and so on, than members of any other species; but we will not regard as sacrosanct the life of each and every member of our species, no matter how limited its capacity for intelligent or even conscious life may be. If we compare a severely defective human infant with a non-human animal, a dog or a pig, for example, we will often find the non-human to have superior capacities, both actual and potential, for rationality, self-consciousness, communication, and anything else that can plausibly be considered morally significant. Only the fact that the defective infant is a member of the species Homo sapiens leads it to be treated differently from the dog or pig. Species membership alone, however, is not morally relevant.[16]

In 1998, Peter Singer was appointed as a tenured member of the Princeton University faculty, where he teaches ethics in the Center for Human Values. Philosophy professor Peter Unger, of New York University, in a letter to *The Wall Street Journal*, wrote, "by many measures, he's the most influential ethicist alive."

You can be sure Mr. Singer's views are held by many educated and influential persons of the modern West, who have been taught to view man as a product of natural evolution, the result of the random coming together of amino acids in sea water, having no real value or meaning beyond that which we decide for ourselves, or someone else decides for us. This is what Singer refers to as "our better understanding of our own nature." Here the distinction between human and non-human has no basis at all, for man and animal are essentially the same, distinguished only by species. And, as Singer says, "Species membership alone is not morally relevant."

According to Singer's "better understanding," a person's significance is determined by one's capacity for rationality, self-consciousness, communication, and so on. People, whether infants or the aged, who do not meet the minimum standards of capacity in these areas have less value than a healthy pig. On June 24, 1999, in an interview with PBS, Mr. Singer declared, "Killing a newborn baby, whether able-bodied or not, I think, is never equivalent to killing a being who wants to go on living... The cases where it is not wrong are those cases where the parents and doctors decide that the child shall not live." And on October 2, 1999, the *Washington Times* quoted Mr. Singer as saying, "Killing a defective infant is not morally equivalent to killing a person. Sometimes it is not wrong at all."

The outcome of such thinking has very serious ramifications for those whose mental or physical capacities are impaired. If people are eliminated because they are seen as not being significant enough, due to physical or mental limitations, then who will determine what degree of imperfection is not perfect enough to warrant living?

This question should sober us to the core. Carried to its logical conclusion, the elimination of people – whether handicapped or not – who are considered insignificant on the basis that they fail to measure up to someone else's idea of what is significant, could someday very well put every one of us at risk.

## THE MYSTERIOUS POWER OF THE POWERLESS

Oliver deVinck was born in 1947. He was one of those people who would not have met Peter Singer's minimum standards of moral significance. His brother, Christopher, an English teacher, wrote about him in an article which appeared in *The Wall Street Journal*, April 10, 1985. This is his story:

I grew up in the house where my brother was on his back in his bed for thirty-two years, in the same corner of his room, under the same window, beside the same yellow walls. He was blind, mute. His legs were twisted. He didn't have the strength to lift his head nor the intelligence to learn anything. Oliver was born with severe brain damage which left him and his body in a permanent state of helplessness. Today I am an English teacher, and each time I introduce my class to the play about Helen Keller, The Miracle Worker, I tell my students the story about Oliver.

One day, during my first year of teaching, I was trying to describe Oliver's lack of response, how he had been spoon-fed every morsel he ever ate, how he never spoke. A boy in the last row raised his hand and said, "Oh, Mr. deVinck. You mean he was a vegetable." I stammered for a few seconds. My family and I fed Oliver. We changed his diapers, hung his clothes and bed linen on the basement line in the winter, and spread them out white and clean on the lawn in the summer. I always liked to watch the grasshoppers jump on the pillowcases.

We bathed Oliver. We tickled his chest to make him laugh. Sometimes we left the radio on in his room. We pulled the shade down over his bed in the morning to keep the sun from burning his tender skin. We listened to him laugh as we watched television downstairs. We listened to him rock his arms up and down to make the bed squeak. We listened to him cough in the middle of the night.

"Well, I guess you could call him a vegetable. I called him Oliver, my brother. You would have loved him." One afternoon, a few months after he was born, my mother brought Oliver to a window. She held him there in the sun, the bright good sun, and there Oliver looked and looked directly into the sunlight, which was the first moment my mother realized that Oliver was blind.

My parents, the true heroes of this story, learned, with the passing of months, that Oliver could not hold up his head, could not crawl, walk, sing; he could not hold anything in his hand; he could not speak. So they brought Oliver to Mt. Sinai Hospital in New York City for tests to determine the extent of his condition. Dr. DeLang said that he wanted to make it very clear to both my mother and father that there was absolutely nothing that could be done for Oliver. He didn't want my parents to grasp at false hope. "You could place him in an institution," he said. "But," my parents replied, "he is our son. We will take Oliver home, of course." The good doctor said, "Then take him home and love him."

Oliver grew to the size of a ten-year-old. He had a big chest, a large head. His hands and feet were those of a five year old, small and soft. We'd wrap a box of baby cereal for him at Christmas and place it under the tree, pat his head with a damp cloth in the middle of a July heat wave. His baptismal certificate hung on the wall above his head. A bishop came to the house and confirmed him.

Oliver still remains the most hopeless human being I ever met, the weakest human being I ever met, and yet he was one of the most powerful human beings I ever met. Oliver could do absolutely nothing except breathe, sleep, eat, and yet he was responsible for action, love, courage, insight. I remember my mother saying when I was small, "Isn't it wonderful that you can see?" And once she said, "When you go to heaven, Oliver will run to you, embrace you, and the first thing he will say is 'Thank you.'"

I remember, too, my mother explaining to me that we were blessed with Oliver in ways that were not clear to her at first. So often parents are faced with a child who is severely retarded but who is also hyperactive, demanding, or wild, who needs constant care. So many people have little choice but to place their child in an institution. Each circumstance is different. No one can judge.

When I was in my early twenties I met a girl and fell in love. After a few months I brought her home to meet my family. After the introductions, the small talk my mother went to the kitchen to check the meal, and I asked the girl, "Would you like to see Oliver?" for I had, of course, told her about my brother. "No," she answered.

Soon after, I met Roe, a lovely girl. She asked me the names of my brothers and sisters. She loved children. I thought she was wonderful. I brought her home after a few months to meet my family. Then it was time for me to feed Oliver.

I remember sheepishly asking Roe if she'd like to see him. "Sure," she said, and up the stairs we went. I sat at Oliver's bedside as Roe watched over my shoulder. I gave him his first spoonful, his second. "Can I do that?" Roe asked with ease, with freedom, with compassion, so I gave her the bowl, and she fed Oliver one spoonful at a time. The power of the powerless. Which girl would you marry? Today Roe and I have three children.*

What possible value could there be in human impairment? Oliver deVinck's brother understood. Oliver, one of the most physically and mentally impaired persons possible, a person many would say had no significance whatsoever, a "vegetable" by some people's definition, became a very significant teacher, mover of minds, giver of insight, instiller of courage, and motivator of genuine love. He deeply impacted a future English teacher, a future husband and father, and a future writer who was able to pass on Oliver's impact to thousands of others in *The Wall Street Journal* on April 10, 1985. And today, perhaps Oliver has touched your life as well.

The answer to the question of value in human impairment often lies not so much in what the impaired can do *for* those around them, but what they can do *in* those around them. This is the mysterious power of the powerless. God using the weak ones of this world to do a significant work in those of us who think we're not impaired, but may be more impaired on the inside than we realize.

There is another important lesson for us in the story of Oliver deVinck, having to do with the identity of children. Namely, their identity is not to be found in what they do, but in who they are. Oliver deVinck could never become a person. He was born a person. There was absolutely nothing Oliver deVinck could do to authenticate his personhood. Yet neither can anyone else. For human personhood is not something dependent upon one's abilities, performance, or age. It is a gift people possess, a state of being which comes with life, no matter what stage of development, be it embryo, toddler, teenager, or aged adult. It is not something children lose when they behave like an animal or gain when they behave like a mature adult. Personhood simply cannot be achieved or lost.

While certainly there is a process of maturity people go through, at no point along the continuum of life can we say a person is less a person than at any other point. A toddler is fully toddler, just as much as a middle-aged adult is fully middle-aged, and both are fully human, both are fully persons.

---

* Excerpt from *The Power of the Powerless* by Christopher deVinck. Copyright 1988 by Christopher deVinck. Reprinted by permission of Christopher deVinck.

What is the basis of personhood? It is based on God's law of reproduction of life after its own kind. Because of this law, people beget people. It can be no other way. A child is born a person because its mother and father are persons. And the child's parents are persons because their parents were persons, and so on back through the lineage of personhood to the parents of all persons: Adam and Eve. On what basis can we say Adam and Eve were persons? On the basis that God created them in the likeness of Himself, the one and only personal God.

Man has no basis for personhood apart from a lineage back to Eden, to the source of personhood in God Himself. Cutting himself off from the original Father, contemporary man has successfully severed himself from any basis of identity beyond that of a colossal cosmic accident, possessing only whatever relative value society may or may not choose to give him.

It must be clearly understood that the biblical model of the child presents us with an entirely personal being of a totally different kind than any other living thing. All children must then be seen as special creations of divine origin and endowment. They must be accepted as individuals whose place in the world and personal worth is securely established by who they are, not by what they may someday become. The point is this: Children do not have to achieve anything to earn our utmost respect. They do not have to grow up to become people of value. They do not need to prove themselves. They must be regarded as persons of full value from the moment of conception, not on the basis of looks, strength, or intelligence, but on the basis of creation alone.

### HEBREW "FAMILY VALUES"

A father bore a son,
and this son bore a son.
That son bore a son,
and a son plus ten.
And from the twelve a nation did come.

The phenomenon of Israel is a family phenomenon. The history of the Jews begins with a single father, Abraham, who was the first to be called a Hebrew, and proceeds from there, across thousands of years, through many trials and hardships, to the present day. Throughout the history of Israel, family has played a fundamental role in their ongoing strength and preservation.

In ancient Israel, it was the family which served as the basic building block of their society. This is in stark contrast to the ancient Greeks, who, as we have seen, built with different blocks. For the Spartans, it was the army barrack. For the Athenians, a headlong pursuit of cultural individualism brought about an ancient women's liberation movement, accompanied by a devaluing of motherhood. Fatherhood was also devalued, as evidenced by the fact that in some cities, during the latter stages of Greece, as few as one family in twelve had two sons, and hardly any had daughters.

It is widely recognized that the Hebrews were a society that greatly valued family. But the question is, why was family so important to them? What assumptions lie behind this?

First, Hebrew parents viewed children as entrusted to them by God, and received them as such into their households like divine appointments. Unlike the Athenians, who had ten days to decide whether or not to formally accept a newborn into the family, the Hebrews took all comers. Even under the most difficult of circumstances and in the most trying of times, a child was received into the household as from the Lord.

Such was the case when Israel was enslaved by Egypt. Socially and economically, this was one of the darkest hours of Hebrew history. They were utter slaves in the land, having taskmasters over them deliberately trying to do all they could to make their lives bitter (Exodus 1:11-14). While there are those today who might look at these circumstances and question parents for the bearing of children into such a difficult life, the Israelites multiplied all the more in the face of tribulation. As recorded in verse 12, "the more [the Egyptians] afflicted them, the more they multiplied." And they refused to practice the killing of infants, even when commanded to do so by Pharaoh, because they "feared [or revered] God, that He established households [or made families] for them" (Ex. 1:21).

Seeing children as from the Lord for the purpose of establishing households also explains why the Hebrews were forbidden to practice the sacrificing of children to idols. While surrounding nations practiced it, the word of the Lord to Moses required that any man who sacrificed his offspring to the heathen god Molech "shall surely be put to death; the people of the land shall stone him with stones" (Leviticus 20:2).

A second assumption behind the strength of the Hebrew household was the acceptance of the idea that it was a father's duty to take an active role in the instruction of children in the home. Because of this commonly practiced expectation, ancient Israel earned its reputation as a strongly patriarchal society, and it was Abraham himself who set the standard for generations to follow. Do you remember the time, in Genesis 18, when Abraham invited the Lord to join him for a barbecue at the oaks of Mamre? We noted earlier how unusually personal Abraham's relationship was with the Lord. God shared His thoughts with Abraham in a remarkably intimate way.

Genesis 18:19 gives us a hint regarding God's motive for sharing Himself with Abraham in such a personal and direct manner. It seems God's reason in allowing Abraham to know Him like he did was to motivate Abraham to take an active and direct role in his own family, teaching his household as God had taught him, with the goal in mind that those who followed would become a morally responsible people and a great and mighty nation: "For I have known him, in order that he may command his children and his household after him, that they keep the way of the Lord, to do righteousness and justice, that the Lord may bring to Abraham what He has spoken to him." (NKJ)

There was something in Abraham God needed to build upon in order for a great and mighty nation to become a reality: a parental mentor, a father who would "command his children after him," rearing a God-honoring household, which would in turn rear another, and another, and another. Of course this does not minimize the role of the mother. The Proverbs have much to say about her as well. But the fact remains, the biblical model clearly places the primary responsibility for the initiation of moral instruction of children upon the shoulders of fathers in the context of their own homes. The Apostle Paul spoke directly to the issue in Ephesians 6:4: "And you, fathers bring [your children] up in the training and admonition of the Lord." He also made it clear that a father who did not rear his children to honor the Lord was not qualified for leadership in the church (2 Timothy 3:4-5).

A third assumption contributing to strong families in Israel, was the understanding that children were not the center of the home. This may seem at first hearing to be a somewhat contradictory statement, but it is not. Although children were received as entrustments from God, and valued accordingly, they were to be trained from the earliest years to realize that life did not revolve around themselves. This realization was brought about through training in respectful obedience to parents, and the honoring of them in their position of authority.

In training children to honor their father and mother, Hebrew parents were laying a foundation of honor for God and respect for others which could be laid in no more effective way. Through the practice of obedience to parental authority, it was impressed upon the minds and hearts of children that there was a higher will above their own, to which they must honorably and respectfully submit.

If children could learn to respect and obey the objective, higher will of a father and mother while they were still children in the context of the household, how much easier it would be to obey the objective, higher will of God as adults in the context of the broader community. Perhaps this explains why Jewish sages have traditionally linked the Fifth Commandment, "Honor your father and mother," to the first four commandments, which have to do with one's relationship to God rather than with the last five commandments that have to do with man's relationship with other men.

So vital was this issue of respect for parental authority, that in ancient Israel a parent was given the right to bring a rebellious child before the elders of the city for the penalty of death through stoning (Deut. 21:18-21). This may be shocking to those today who have been led to accept the assumption that teenage rebellion is a normal and expected part of growing up. But it was not normal and expected in ancient Israel. (We will say more about this later as we seek to understand why this was true.)

While a child-centered home was not the Hebrew model of a household, you can be sure it was no stranger to Athens. One of the most powerful and influential rulers of Athens was a man named Themistocles (the-mis'-to-klez). He was a general who had command of the entire Athenian army. The Greek historian Plutarch gave us a little peek into his home life when he wrote these words: "Of his son, who was pert towards his mother, [Themistocles] said that the boy wielded more power than anybody else in Greece; for the Athenians ruled the Greeks, he himself ruled the Athenians, the boy's mother ruled himself, and the boy ruled the mother." [17] To make such a statement in Israel, even in jest, would have been shameful. It was their view that it was a curse to be ruled by women and children.

The Israelites did not put their confidence in youth, nor did they hail the younger generation as "the hope of the future," that is, in the sense of looking to youth for innovative answers or fresh new outlooks on life. Such a hope wants to believe the next generation will succeed where the older generation has failed. It is the longing expectancy that youth will somehow rise up and win battles where defeat has previously been the norm.

Perhaps this consoling dream is the adult world's way of finding solace from the realities of an inadequate present, or relieving themselves of their own sense of responsibility for solutions. But whatever the reason, the exaltation of youth and looking to them for answers was foreign to the Hebrews. The exaltation of youth is, however, one of the distinguishing marks of the twentieth-century West.

Historian Paul Johnson noted that vigorous appeals to youth for answers to major social problems began to take place in Europe during the early years of the twentieth century on the part of pre-World War I politicians:

Youth movements were a European phenomenon, especially in Germany where 25,000 members of the Wandervogel clubs hiked, strummed guitars, protested about pollution and the growth of cities, and damned the old. Opinion-formers like Max Weber and Arthur Moeller van den Bruck demanded that youth be brought to the helm. The nation, wrote Bruck, "needs a change of blood, an insurrection of the sons against the fathers, a substitution of the old by the young." All over Europe, sociologists were assiduously studying the youth to find out what they thought and wanted. And, of course, what the youth wanted was war.[18]

As for ancient Israel, the hope of the future did not rest in the hands of youth, but rather rested firmly upon the shoulders of fathers as heads of families and elders as heads of communities. Elders did not look to youth for wisdom, neither were youth to look to their peers for understanding. Hebrew children were to honor their parents and elders for a very good reason – the hope of their future rested in adult hands. For better or for worse, as went the fathers, so went the nation. If the younger generation was to enter into wisdom and blessing, it was the fathers who would lead them there. Herein lay the real hope of the future: that the hearts of fathers would turn to their children, and the hearts of children would then respond to their fathers (see Malachi 4:5).

Israel was definitely an elder-oriented society. The Hebrews did not elevate youth, nor did they exalt the child. On the contrary, they venerated age. It was an attitude that stood in striking contrast to ancient Athens, which treated age unkindly, and may account for the fact Athenians feared and mourned old age.

A fourth contributing factor to the strength of the Hebrew family was the understanding that the individual family was but a part of something much larger than itself: a community with a common history, a joint destiny, and shared values mutually applied. Hebrew children, as well as their parents, were repeatedly reminded of their common unity with other Hebrew families through the observance of various festivals, feasts, and times of remembrance. Their corporate identity as one nation under God was not to be lost or forgotten. Public readings of Scripture were a part of their coming together, in which they were reminded of their history and the place of God in their lives. An awareness of who they were as a people, and from whence they had come, was to be regularly inculcated upon young minds and hearts. Memorials of historic events in which God showed Himself faithful to them were put in place so that when their children and grandchildren asked, "What is this all about?" parents would have another opportunity to instruct and remember.

The strength of Israel's common unity was not found through political or cultural means, as was attempted in Athens. And unlike Sparta, although they were at times brought together for military purposes, it was not the army that provided the primary bond. The real strength of Israel was found in something beyond the individual family, the neighborhood, the city, the tribe, and even the nation itself. The center of it all, whether family, city, or state, was found in this familiar and often heard cry, known to Jews as the Shema (literally "Hear!"): "Hear, O Israel. The Lord is our God, the Lord is one! And you shall love the Lord your God with all your heart and with all your soul and with all your might" (Deut. 6:4-5).

The ultimate center was not the king, nor the elders at the gate, nor the father in the home, nor priest or prophet, nor athletics, the arts, youth, education, or philosophy, but something above it all: the one and only personal and unlimited living God, who had revealed Himself in words they could comprehend, and to whom they were equally accountable, both young and old, parent and child, common man or monarch, and on whom they were to focus their love and service. Place a family in this kind of setting, and the results will speak for themselves.

## THE DUTY OF THE HEBREW PARENT

Have you ever seen one of those drawings with the caption that reads: "What's wrong with this picture?" As you read the following true story of an American high school principal's approach to student life, try looking at the scene with an Hebraic eye, and ask yourself, "What's wrong with this picture?":

The school's principal elaborated on why freedom of choice is so important. Adolescence, he suggested, is a time of normal disorganization; it is therefore psychologically counterproductive to impose restrictions on teenagers. "Freedom is a major learning experience. We don't believe in restraining kids. We want to give them choices with support, and let them make mistakes."

People learn better, he thought, from encountering trouble than they do from smooth sailing. Trouble helps focus attention on problems of morality and justice. It is healthy for teenagers to be exposed to the admittedly unhealthy things that sometimes happen in school, such as vandalism and snowball fights. "The school represents these paradoxes rather than attempts to control them," the principal said. During Dr. Nelson's celebration of freedom he was informed that his son's locker had just been blown up.[19]

Dr. Nelson's aversion to restraining teenagers is totally understandable. By the time a young man or woman reaches high school, he or she should have sparse need for restraint. By this time, the disciplines should be internally self-imposed, not externally imposed by others. But here is the problem: American high schools are made up of large numbers of students whose parents have used Dr. Nelson's non-restraining approach at home from nearly day one, and consequently Johnny never did learn one of the most important skills in life: self-control.

A man or woman, boy or girl, with self-control operative in his or her life is a person who can be trusted with freedom. The more internal control a person has, the more he or she may be free of external control. The Scriptures tell us that a person who controls his own self is stronger than a man who captures an entire city (Proverbs 16:32). How rare it is today.

Where does self-control come from? Are some people just born with a bent toward internal discipline while others are not? Or is it something that can be acquired and developed in anyone? In this chapter, we will attempt to clarify that self-control is an acquired trait, which does not come about "naturally" in people, but can be developed in children. We will also clarify that external discipline from parents in the lives of young children is for the purpose of producing internal discipline in teenagers and adults of later life.

We are presently living at a time when many parents view anything but the most minimal forms of restraint, restriction, or external control, as impositions upon the child's development, and therefore psychologically counterproductive. Parents fear lest they will somehow warp their offspring. Such a parent may say, like Dr. Nelson, "The toddler years are a time of normal disorganization; it is therefore psychologically counterproductive to impose restrictions on toddlers... I don't believe in restraining them." And then a little later, "Childhood is a time of normal disorganization; it is therefore psychologically counterproductive to impose restrictions on children. I don't believe in restraining children."

But why have many of today's parents come to accept the assumption that it is psychologically counterproductive to impose restrictions on children? It comes, in part, from a misguided belief in the noble purity, inherent goodness, and innocence of children. It also comes from the idea that children, allowed to mature "naturally," with the least amount of imposition, will "naturally" develop into their best selves. It seems to be part of the modern "back to nature" movement. Natural foods and natural kids.

Parents who operate out of this assumption will allow their children to behave "naturally," giving "free expression" to their thoughts and emotions, with a bare minimum of parental interference. Discipline beyond the minimum necessary for health and safety, will be viewed as detrimental and stifling to the flowering of a child's true self.

Such parents are directed by a policy of non-direction, often viewing a child's freedom in terms of letting him do his own thing, or, "becoming his own man." We live in a day when self-expression is valued above self-control. Behavior others view as uncouth will be excused by such parents with a shrug of the shoulders, and, "That's just the way he is," or, "He's going through a very normal stage of rebellion, what do you expect?"

This view of children finds no support whatsoever from the Scriptures. Yes, children are special creations of divine origin, made in the likeness of God, bearing His image, having innate value, worthy of our utmost respect, and to be treated with the greatest dignity. But, at the same time, even in the most angelic of children there is a fallen nature inherent to mankind. This is what allows them to be so thoughtless or cruel to others at times, willfully defiant to parents, or downright obnoxious in grocery stores. This explains why it is that not having been taught to lie, some are able to do it so well. Teachers do not teach them to cheat, yet some become experts in the field! (Ask Dr. Nelson. He knows.)

As unpopular as it may be to suggest that children are naturally flawed, it is consistent with the biblical view of fallen man. Though not the way God originally made him to be, it is nonetheless the way he now is. The fact is, children are basically foolish, intrinsically self-seeking, and in need of an alteration of their natural, normal, unrestrained behavior. So, enter parents!

To accept the assumption that children are in need of a basic change from their natural, normal, state is fundamental to the Hebrew mentality of parenthood. Through this window, children are seen as being naturally foolish, not naturally wise. Wisdom is not something which comes naturally to a child. It is something which must be acquired from outside the individual, while foolishness is something to be removed from within, with parents playing a central role in this process of exchange.

Parents who understand this recognize their responsibility and obligation to mold and shape their children's sense of what is appropriate and inappropriate behavior, and what is right or wrong. It is the role of parents to provide the external discipline necessary to bring about internal discipline in their children. Responsible parenting calls children up to a standard they would not otherwise enter into by themselves.

Hebrew parents would not have been satisfied with the modern notion that children should just "be themselves." "A child who gets his own way [literally, 'left to himself']" says Proverbs 29:15, "brings shame to his mother." It was not up to children to clarify their own value system, or to determine moral truths by looking within themselves. Rather, it was the parents' duty to clarify for their children what God had already clarified for them.

As much as this flies in the face of our postmodern free choice ethic of "every man doing what is right in his own eyes," it is clearly the biblical model.

And there are rich rewards for those parents who heed God's instruction, and begin the process very early in the lives of their children.

A successful college professor chose to leave his university post to teach elementary students. His fellow college profs couldn't understand why he would give up his prestigious position to teach young children. It seemed like too great a step down. But his response said it all: "Would you rather write your name in brick before it's baked, or afterward?"

When it comes to molding and shaping, it works a lot better when the clay is soft. And when it comes to fulfilling the parental duty to mold and shape a child's sense of ethics and internal discipline, working with the clay while it's still soft is essential.

There is a good reason humans take so long to mature. In the animal world, a horse is up and walking within hours. Many animals are fully independent within weeks or months. But in our culture, most human offspring don't leave home for eighteen years! A seventy-two-year-old man or woman has spent twenty-five percent of his or her lifetime in the "growing up" stage. That's a very long proportionate time.

But this time has a special purpose for humans, which is not necessary for animals. It is a time for parent-child relationship building, through which the duty of parental training and equipping of children is accomplished. It is a time for the molding and shaping of attitudes and character. It is time for building a sense of ethics and morality into the heart of the next generation. It is a time for youth to learn the internal discipline of self-control.

Parents who wait until their children are teenagers to build the proper relationship necessary to mold and shape the clay have missed the twelve prime years God intended for this to be happening. This is really unfortunate, because it's always harder to work with half-baked bricks. Rebellion is something not easily dealt with in teenagers. But, it can (and must) be properly and effectively confronted at the age of two and three.

Parents who do so are being proactive. To be proactive means to take action before hand. It is the kind of action that seeks to minimize or eliminate reactive problems and stress later on. Proactive parents prepare their children ahead of time. The process begins when children are very young, so that by the time they reach the teen years, reactive parenting is not taking place.

The difference between being proactive and reactive can be illustrated through an educational example. Imagine yourself as the teacher of a class of

25 third-graders in a school that has fire drills on a regular basis. Knowing that a drill is certain to take place, you take proactive measures to insure your students will exit the building in a safe and orderly way. You not only tell your class what to do in case of a fire drill, but you train them through guided practice in preparation for the event to come, prior to its arrival. Before the day the alarm sounds, you and your class have already walked through the requirements of a safe exit. Johnny has practiced closing the windows, Joan has practiced turning off the lights, and you have practiced being the last one out of the room and closing the door behind you. The students have mastered the skill of walking in an orderly line to a designated spot outside the building.

All this is done so that when the alarm sounds, all goes well. No confusion. No panic, and, wonder of wonders, no "normal disorganization." But you can be sure if you had not done your proactive part to train the class, normal disorganization would have been the natural result, and reactive stress would have dramatically gripped you when the alarm sounded!

Rabbi Donin, in *To Raise a Jewish Child*, comments on the role of parents as teachers in the Hebrew tradition:

The Hebrew word for parents (*horim*) and for teachers (*morim*) are similar. They sound the same. They mean the same. Both words mean to instruct, to teach. Parents and teachers are listed together in the same passage of the confessional recited on Yom Kippur (Al Het): "For the sin that we have sinned before Thee is belittling parents and teachers." They are listed together, not to save space, but because the Jewish heritage has traditionally linked their roles. The parent's role as teacher of his children is continually stressed in Jewish sources.[20]

Please note that the Hebrew word for parent means to instruct, to teach. Parenting skills, therefore, are teaching skills, and to be a parent is to be a teacher.

Not only do extra-biblical Jewish sources emphasize the teaching role of parents, but the Bible itself is direct on this matter. Parents were instructed to teach the words of the Lord diligently to their children as they sat in their house, walked along the way, went to bed, and when they got up in the morning (Deuteronomy 6:4-9). That pretty well covered a day. And they were also instructed to make the wonders of the Lord known to their children and to their grandchildren (Deut. 4:9-10). That pretty well covered a lifetime.

When it comes to imparting truth to the hearts and minds of children, the home is the primary schoolhouse. Only parents have the opportunity to do what is described in Deuteronomy chapter 6. And the entire family benefits.

It is important to note that parents are not just to talk of the Word to their children, but first to be modeling the truth of that Word by the fact that they love the Lord with all their soul and might themselves: "You shall love the Lord… and you shall teach…." Parents who desire their children to embrace the ways of the Lord and yet violate those ways themselves are working against themselves. What they are really teaching is not what they are telling, but rather what they are doing. To know the way of the Lord, in a truly biblical sense, is not to simply intellectually comprehend it, but to actually live it. Therefore, for parents to really teach His ways, they must be practicing His ways. The father who tells his children to respect authority while breaking the speed limit, making U-turns in forbidden spots, or parking in unauthorized zones is making much more of an impact by what is done than by what is said. Training is taking place, in a negative sense, like it or not.

Parents must understand they are teachers no matter whether they lead their children in formal Bible study or not. Instruction cannot be avoided. Children watch, listen, and learn from Dad and Mom on a daily basis, and they will learn no matter what, one way or another. It is simply the nature of the parent-child relationship. If parents do not train their children to acknowledge God they will, through default, train them to ignore Him. Training will take place in the home. The question is simply a matter of what kind.

**CHAPTER FOUR SUMMARY: KEY PEOPLE, PLACES AND CONCEPTS**
Adolf Hitler (1889-1945)
Nazi Germany
Infant Doe
Oliver deVinck
The biblical versus secular basis of human worth
Innate worth, inherent worth
Euthanasia
$QL = NE \times (H+S)$
The biblical basis of personhood
Personhood versus maturity
Bearing the image of Adam

Proactive parenting versus reactive parenting
Telling instead of training
Deuteronomy 6:1-7

*For Further Thought and Discussion*

1. Summarize the similarities between Sparta and Nazi Germany, and between Athens and present-day America.

2. Identify the basic assumptions which underlie the idea that abortion is a woman's "right."

3. Discuss the underlying assumptions which led Peter Singer to conclude that being a member of the species Homo sapiens is not morally relevant. How might Mr. Singer define the word moral?

4. Explain this statement: "In [the evolutionary] view of life neither parents nor children can possibly be personal at all." What is the significance of modern man "de-fathering" himself of God?

5. If people reject a personal lineage back to Adam, and thus back to God, on what basis will they determine the uniqueness of man or the personhood of people?

6. Consider what actions evolutionary thought has led to today.

7. In the story of Oliver deVinck, why do you think the first girlfriend mentioned by Christopher deVinck did not want to see Oliver?

8. Can you give an example of a handicapped person who has moved others to action? Do you know anyone who has been moved to positive action by handicapped people? If so, how has their example affected you?

9. What specific evidence can you cite which would support the notion that child-centered parenting and a youth-centered society are commonly accepted ideas in our current culture?

10. Select current newspaper or magazine articles regarding child-rearing and/or discipline, and analyze them in light of the Hebrew model of child training.

11. List as many specific assumptions as you can which illustrate the contrasting differences between ancient Hebrew and modern Western views of children and parenting. For example: an ancient Hebrew assumption was that rebellion in youth is abnormal, and not to be accepted. A contemporary Western assumption is that rebellion in youth is normal, and to be accepted.

# Chapter Five

# Why the Hebrews
# Were Poor Philosophers

⚜

B efore continuing our inspection of the foundations of Western thought, let's take a moment to recap the highlights of what we have discovered so far. We began by comparing and contrasting Greek and Hebrew views of origin, pointing out the important difference between the idea of life making itself, as the expression of self-creating Mother Nature, and life being made by a cause outside of itself, as the expression of a transcendent Father God; we saw the uniqueness of this personal-yet-unlimited God, and distinguished Him from the personal-yet-limited gods of Mt. Olympus and the unlimited-yet-impersonal god of Nature (capital N), to which many people in our present culture are still paying tribute.

We examined the distinctiveness of man, and differentiated him from the animals as one being created in the likeness and image of the personal God, as opposed to the Greek notion that man is but a rational animal; we noted man's innate basis of worth, as an image-bearer of the worthy Creator, in contrast to the Greeks who based human value upon socially determined factors; we discussed the fact the Hebrews had an objective, non-negotiable, God-given standard of measurement for morality, while the Greeks measured their morality by subjective, society-centered standards, relative to city-state or individual preferences.

We ascertained the Greeks regulated their thinking by independent reason, while the Hebrews regulated their thought by Revelation; we defined two very different concepts of freedom: one which seeks to obliterate boundaries, and the other which seeks to recognize them. We briefly touched upon man's mandate to rule over the earth, under God, and we in turn saw how man has managed to make such a mess of things as a result of the Fall.

We affirmed the inherent value of children as persons to be handled with utmost dignity, as fellow image-bearers of God, yet at the same time being intrinsically self-seeking and in need of a change in their natural, normal behavior; we described the Hebrew model of the home as being not child-centered, but rather God-centered, with fathers taking the initiative in passing on biblical ethics to coming generations, in contrast to the Greeks, whose families were centered in anything but the living God, if they had a family at all.

We now turn our attention toward the enormous influence of Greek philosophy upon the West, and how it has continued to shape our assumptions to the present day. We will begin with a simple word association game. Listed below are the names of six well known Greeks and Hebrews. Next to each name, write the first single word that comes to mind describing who they were, or what they did. You may use the same word more than once:

Socrates     _____

Plato     _____

Aristotle     _____

Abraham     _____

Moses     _____

Paul     _____

Of all the words associated with Socrates, Plato, or Aristotle, you can be sure the word philosopher is near the top of the list, right next to the word Greek. However, when it comes to words associated with Abraham, Moses, or Paul, you can be sure the word philosopher is not among them. Why is this? Why did the Hebrews not make good philosophers, and what does this tell you about the difference between Greek and Hebrew thought? To understand the answers, let's go back to the days of Homer.

Homer was a Greek poet, who is thought to have lived some 800 years before Christ. Little is known about him, but the Greeks credited him with having written the first European books. They were epic poems which you can pick up today at your local library, under the titles of Iliad, and Odyssey. Homer made the Olympian gods and goddesses important in his stories, and ignored the primitive gods of early Greece. Later Greeks closely studied Homer's writings and passed them on. Although the stories (mythoi) of the gods went back through verbal tradition much further than Homer, it was Homer who is believed to have first put the stories in written form. Actually, new myths were being created by poets long after Homer left the scene.

Until the latter stages of Greek decay, when traditional Greek religion was rejected by many in favor of Eastern cults, it was generally accepted among the common people that the gods and goddesses really did exist. Furthermore, it was politically incorrect to offend the gods.

Family and city rituals were built around the honoring of gods, in recognition of their power to affect circumstances and events for good or ill. These rituals were passed on through traditional family and city ceremonies, consisting largely of chants, prayers, and food offerings. Custom provided a basis for these rites, which were as varied as the gods themselves.

But around 200 years after Homer, in about 600 B.C., the very existence of the gods was seriously challenged by the ideas of Thales, of Ionia. It was Thales, you may recall, who advocated what some historians have called the "Ionian Science of Nature," which was a revolutionary new way of thinking about reality in which the gods played no role at all, and Nature accounted for everything. The gods, goddesses, or spirits of any kind were not only unnecessary, but nonexistent. For the first time in history, the supernatural was dismissed from discussion, and secular thought was born.

Perhaps it was inevitable that it would someday happen. Although they were believed to have superhuman powers, the gods of Greek mythology suffered from human-like limitations. As a matter of fact, it was this human-likeness that led Greek philosophers to abandon belief. One such Greek, Xenophanes, made this bold statement: "If horses or oxen had hands and could draw or make statues, horses would represent the forms of the gods like horses, oxen like oxen." In other words, the gods were nothing more than the product of human imagination, created in the likeness and image of men; too human to be divine, too unbelievable to be real.

It was the Ionian nature-philosophers who opened the door to an ancient "gods-are-dead" movement which produced a whole new era of Greek speculation about the true nature of reality. Thales' shift in thought opened the door to such a wide world of speculation that he is sometimes called the Father of Western Philosophy.

With the rejection of the gods came the need for new explanations to account for the mysteries of life and to provide some sort of framework for ethics. A new faith was needed to replace old beliefs. If the gods were not really real, what was? A search for better answers than mythology could provide gave fuel to the driving force behind all Greek philosophy: the quest to know what was really real.

With the Ionian theory of naturalism, and the resultant breakdown of traditional Greek religion, there was little constraint on the rising tide of speculative ideas. Greece, as you may recall, had no sacred writings or divine codes to regulate its thought. The quest to know what was "really real" ranged from the physical world to the metaphysical, from ethics and morality to origins and politics. Debates formed around what was really "good," and what was not, to what was really "best for society," and what was not, and on, and on. With human reason as its starting point and guiding light, Greek philosophy seemed to know no end to its speculative expressions.

By now it may be clear to you why the Hebrews did not make good philosophers. Greek philosophy involved the pursuit of wisdom by the light of human reason, and was quite different from Hebraic religion, which was the pursuit of wisdom by the light of divine revelation. One looked to precepts already provided, while the other looked to provide its own precepts.[21]

The Hebrews did not go through a cultural crisis of theology, as the Greeks did. The God of the Hebrews was never suggested by their leaders to be the imaginative invention of poets, created in the image of man. He continued to be viewed as a living, personal, communicating God who demonstrated His presence and power over and over again in the lives of real people in history. His acts were seen by thousands of witnesses, in fact by millions of witnesses, as in the case of the deliverance from Egypt. The Hebrews did not spend time questioning His existence. Their questions had to do with what He required of their existence.

The difference between Greek philosophy and Hebrew religion can be seen in these comments by Abram Sachar, in A History of the Jews: "To seek God was the ultimate wisdom [for the Hebrew], to follow His precepts the ultimate virtue. The Greek accepted no revelation as ultimate... [He] bowed to no law but that of complete self-expression... Where the Hebrew asked: 'What must

I do?' the Greek asked, 'Why must I do it?'"[22] Abraham Heschel said it this way: "The Greeks learned in order to comprehend. The Hebrews learned in order to revere."[23]

As for any speculation about what was "really real," the very question must have sounded absurd to the ancient believing Jew. After all, God had really called Abraham to be the father of a great nation (of which every Jew was a living part), really delivered the people from Egypt, really spoke at Sinai, and really proved Himself faithful and trustworthy. So what was there to speculate about?

Why did philosophy not do well in Israel? Because the "better answers than mythology could provide," which the Greek philosophers sought out, were those the Hebrews believed they had already found.

### PLATO'S SHADOW

Would anyone in his right mind ever say, "What difference does it make what Thomas Edison thought?" Anyone who knows what Thomas Edison thought would not question the fact his thoughts have made an astounding difference in the way you and I live today. Edison thought it was possible to harness electricity to produce light, and he invented the electric light bulb. Edison thought it was possible for a machine to talk, and so he made the phonograph. He thought moving pictures would be nice, and so he developed motion pictures.

All of these ideas, and many more, transformed the twentieth century. Many of Edison's inventions we could hardly imagine living without. They have revolutionized the way we do business, and the way we have fun. And they will continue to affect our children's lives, and the lives of all who follow. Ideas do make a difference! And significant ideas cast much longer shadows than the men or women who originally think them. Such is the case with Edison, and such is the case with Plato.

The shadow of Plato is now over 2,300 years long, and has not faded. His thoughts have perhaps had more affect upon the way Westerners think and act than any single mortal man in history. Unlike Edison, however, we cannot hold an invention in our hand and say, "Plato thought this up." But we can point to ideas, nonetheless, which have led people to make decisions which would not have been made had Plato not perpetuated certain ideas in the first place. Ideas which germinated at the feet of his teacher, Socrates, and after Plato's death, were blended (first with Judaism and later with Christianity) to form a very potent brew as toxic as any the world has known. His philosophy must be understood, because it has had such a lasting affect upon the West.

What were Plato's philosophic assumptions, and how did he arrive at them? Let's go back to the days prior to Plato for a moment, to get a sense of what Greek philosophy had gone through before he arrived on the scene. Remember that Thales and his followers had dismissed the notion of Homer's gods about 600 years B.C., and Plato's ideas were not heard until about 200 years later. By the time he spoke up there had been quite a lot of philosophic speculation about what was "really real," both in the physical realm of nature, as well as the realm of ethics and morality.

With reason as its starting point and guiding light, Greek philosophy flourished. However, being unrestrained in its speculation, it eventually began to flounder as the many voices of conflicting opinion began to have a degenerating effect. There was failure to agree on many basic issues, including the trustworthiness of man's senses and the reliability of human reason. Various philosophers rose up to challenge each other's concepts of truth. Eventually, by the middle of the fifth century B.C., a period of all-around doubt and skepticism settled in. Out of this climate, a school of philosophers emerged called the Sophists, led by Protagoras.

Protagoras was the author of the famous saying, "Man is the measure of all things." He and other Sophists held that to seek universal truths was a vain search for what could never be found. As a result, they turned their attention toward training young men for successful careers, stressing the ultimacy of personal fulfillment, as it was experienced in Athens of that day. Among the first Greeks to teach for pay, they gained a reputation for being materialistically minded.

It was during this period that Socrates came into the picture. He did not want to be connected with the Sophists. His focus of concern was upon non-materialistic concepts such as "goodness," "justice," "virtue," and, "the best way to live." True to Greek form, however, he did not turn to objective revelation for his answers, but leaned on subjective reason. His famous dialectic method of teaching involved asking searching questions of his pupils in a effort to cause them to arrive at their own ideas of the meaning of such things as goodness and justice, forming their own notions of right and wrong in order that they might be able to justify living within their own opinions. This method of clarifying personal values is still used today in many American schools.

Plato, the most famous pupil of Socrates, also reacted to the materialism of the Sophists. He, too, chose not to focus his attention on material things, but to try and find lasting value and significance in the non-material world of ideals. The ideals of Socrates and Plato centered around the recognition of unchanging universals (i.e., universal truths and values) which would give true significance to all of the changing particulars in the material world that came and went with the passing of time. After all, what lasting value could there be in making a lot of money only to buy a big house and fancy togas that would eventually deteriorate and fall apart? Plato's philosophy of metaphysical idealism stressed the value of eternal, perfect, non-deteriorating ideals, in contrast to the temporal, imperfect, and deteriorating things of the physical world.

More than this, Plato actually sought a way of escape from the harsh realities of the present physical world through trance-like meditation on the metaphysical world of ideals. In essence, Plato split reality into two distinct arenas: an upper level of eternal, non-material ideals, and a lower level of temporal, physical matter. The higher aspect of reality was called "form" and the lower level was called "matter." Since the words form and matter are often used in reference to Greek thought, they should be clearly understood.

To understand these concepts, draw a circle on a blank piece of paper. The universal ideal, or concept, of "circle" takes on a particular expression when it is drawn on the piece of paper. But your drawing of a particular circle is only a temporary and imperfect (possibly a very imperfect) representation of the perfect ideal of "circle-ness," which existed prior to your drawing and will continue to exist long after your drawing has gone the way of all drawings. Your sketch of a circle is a concrete, physical expression of an abstract, non-physical ideal, and, according to Plato's philosophy, it is the universal, non-physical ideal ("form") which has a more lasting significance than the particular physical expression of that ideal ("matter") on paper.

In the same way, other "forms" included such ideals as "beauty," "justice," "truth," and "goodness," eternal unchangeables which could only be truly appreciated through contemplation and meditation. For example, one might look at a rose and consider the flower itself to be but a temporary and imperfect expression of a higher form of beauty that does not fade in the heat and turn brown with age. True beauty, for Plato, was a metaphysical concept, eternally unchanging and absolute forever, unaffected by decay. Plato believed the temporal world of matter was far inferior to the "real" world of eternal forms, since the material world consisted only of temporary and imperfect shadows of the true and unchanging world behind it. He thereby established a dualism between two realms – the temporal realm of physical matter and the eternal realm of metaphysical ideals, with the non-physical being superior to the physical.

The outcome of Plato's thought was a devaluing of the physical world and a mystical elevating of the unseen world of ideals and eternal "forms." He downgraded the body, and exalted the soul, calling the body the "prison house of the soul." He, and others like him, honored artists and philosophers while degrading manual labor and those who performed it. This, like so much of Greek thinking, stood in direct opposition to the view of ancient Hebrews, as we will examine next.

## THE PROBLEM WITH PLATO'S DUALISM

Someone aptly said, "The most effective lies are those which come as close to the truth as possible." That's no lie!

In order to understand the far-reaching negative effects of Plato's dualism, we must first acknowledge the parts of the lie that are true. Yes, there are points of agreement between Plato's philosophy and what we read in the Bible. First, both in Plato's philosophy as well as in the Bible, we see a distinction between that which is temporal and that which is eternal. Eternal things are not affected by time. Temporal things are temporary. They do not go on for ever and ever. Whether it's a Ford, a Chevy, or a Rolls Royce, they all end up in the same place. (No, they don't go to car heaven.) Even though the lilies of the field are arrayed more beautifully than Solomon in all his finery, they will wither and pass away, but the Word of God abides forever. One just lasts for a season, while the other for eternity.

Second, both Plato and the prophets understood that you can't take it with you, and it is foolish to try to live life as though you could. A fixation upon the material world of things, storing up for yourself treasures on earth, "where moth and rust corrupt," is shortsighted vanity.

Third, both Plato and the Bible speak of two different aspects of reality – the physical and the non-physical, or, the material and the spiritual. Spiritual things are not affected by time or space.

But although the distinction is there, between the temporal and the eternal, as well as the physical and the spiritual, the Bible does not teach that the temporal, physical world is something to be inherently devalued or downgraded. On the contrary, the physical creation is something God declared to be inherently good. Even in its fallen state, creation is full of God's glory from sea to sky, and He has a purpose for it, even though a temporary one.

Furthermore, while the Bible makes a distinction between the physical world and the spiritual world, it does not teach that the physical world is any less real, or less significant than the spiritual world. On the contrary, both the seen and the unseen, the physical as well as the spiritual are of God, their mutual Maker and Sustainer.

As mentioned before, the Genesis record presents us with a universe fully created through the intelligent commands of the personal and unlimited God who spoke it into existence. All of creation – all that exists – came into being through God's spoken word: "And God said, 'Let there be'... and there was... ." The fact that creation was made real through God's spoken word is an important factor in understanding the biblical view of reality. The Hebrew word for word (*dabhar*) is something more than just spoken sounds of the lip and breath. *Dabhar* is something active, dynamic, moving, and powerful. It incorporates the concept of deed as well as speech. Thus, when God created by means of His word, He was not just speaking out ideas about creation, but actually doing creation through His spoken "word-deed." What God spoke into existence at the first moment of creation continued to exist into the next moment by the authority of that same word-deed. The *dabhar* of God which brought vegetation into reality on the third day of creation continued to hold it together and sustain it on the fourth. And the fifth. And every moment since, including right now.

His word-deed is as active today as it was when He first spoke it out into empty space. His word is still doing, still sustaining, still holding things together. As we said previously, we must not view creation as merely a one-time act of the past, but rather as a continuing deed of the present. It is not as though God made all of creation at some point in the past, and now it exists quite well on its own, functioning "naturally." God's initial act of creation was an awesome deed. Yet His present act of holding it all together is an equally awesome deed. The present is as magnificent as the beginning, the very continuing existence of the universe as remarkable as its first appearance.

God's continuing word-deed is still being heard. It is as clearly audible today as it was on the first day of creation. As the psalmist put it, "The heavens are telling of the glory of God; and their expanse is declaring the work of His hands. Day to day pours forth speech, and night to night reveals knowledge... Their line [sound] has gone out through all the earth, and their utterances to the end of the world" (Psalm 19:1-4). No man can claim ignorance, for "since the creation of the world [God's] invisible attributes, His eternal power and divine nature, have been clearly seen, being understood through what has been made, so that they are without excuse" (Romans 1:20).

In light of all this, any sort of distinction between so-called "natural" and "supernatural" aspects of reality must be carefully reexamined. In terms of how most present day people think about the natural and the supernatural, the natural has come to mean "the normal operation of a self-governing system," while the supernatural refers to "the interference of God in that system." But this concept is unbiblical. In a biblical view of reality, the concept of nature as a self-creating, self-sustaining system must be abandoned. When people with a biblical view of reality consider life around them they cannot legitimately split it up into two kinds of reality, a "natural" kind and a "supernatural" kind, as though God's power were operative in the one while in the other, things function quite "naturally" on their own.

If God spoke vegetation into existence on the third day of creation, and by that same word-deed continues to keep it going today, how then could today's vegetation be considered "natural" at all? That which was not "natural" in the beginning can be no more "natural" today. In The Amplified Bible, Colossians 1:16-17 reads, "For it was in Him that all things were created, in heaven and on earth, things seen and things unseen, whether thrones, dominions, rulers or authorities; all things were created and exist through Him and in Him and for Him. And He Himself existed before all things and in Him all things consist – cohere, are held together." What is "natural" about that? In terms of God's active, sustaining power, there can be no distinction between so-called "natural" and "supernatural" aspects of reality at all. As mentioned earlier, whether it be in an act of raising bread at the local bakery, or raising Lazarus from the dead, God is active and operative in both. While the one event takes place in a customary or ordinary manner, and the other takes place in an unusual or out-of-the-ordinary way, God's power is evident in both. By virtue of His word-deed both the seen and the unseen, both the physical and the spiritual, both the temporal and the eternal, both the miraculous and the routine are real, significant, and share a common unity through His creating-sustaining power. And because of this unifying factor, we are able to call the universe a universe.

We must not err in thinking that somehow the physical aspects of life are second-rate because they are temporary. Different? Yes. Passing away? Yes. But, unimportant? No. Contemptible? God forbid. Having no value? Of course not. Since God made it and continues to sustain it, who is man to degrade it?

Think of it this way. The clothing you wear today will someday be worn out and discarded. But does this mean it has no value or significant purpose in the meantime? Of course not! Try going a day or two without it, and you will soon discover just how valuable, wonderful, and significant it really is. Of course this does not imply that a person's blue jeans are as precious as a person's soul. The one Jesus died to preserve eternally, while the other has only a short-lived earth-bound importance.

The point here is simply that the God of the Bible is the God of the physical as well as the God of the spiritual, the God of the seen as well as the God of the unseen, the God of the temporal as well as the God of the eternal. He is equally Lord of both at once. Furthermore, He is fulfilling His purposes in both the perishable as well as the imperishable. To imply that His work is of value in the eternal realm and valueless in the temporary realm is to fall short of appreciating His full purposes for both a temporary earth as well as an eternal heaven. He is out to do His will in both.

Why are we spending so much time on this point? Because there is a tendency among Christians to value the eternal, spiritual aspects of reality so much that they get off balance by devaluing or downgrading the temporal, physical world of the here and now. This has never been a hallmark of Hebraic thought, either in Scripture or Jewish tradition. On the contrary, the Hebrew model affirms the physical world with vigor and thanksgiving.

Instead of elevating the soul and downplaying the body, the Hebrews sought to worship God fully in and through both, seeing God as One to be loved and served not only with all their heart and mind, but with all their physical strength as well. The idea of the body being like a prison from which the soul was to be freed was foreign to their thinking.

They did not seek an escape from the present physical world. They sought to know God and do His will within it, while they had the opportunity. The mandate of Genesis 1:27-28 is certainly not a call to deny the physical world, or to endure it until heaven, but to responsibly embrace and care for it. Furthermore, we can find much God-given pleasure, enjoyment and fulfillment of soul in our interaction with the physical world. Marvin Wilson, Professor of Biblical and Theological Studies at Gordon College, made this intriguing observation about the Jewish affirmation of, rather than denial of, the physical world in this present life: "If we find enjoyment in the here and now (see Eccl. 3:12-13) we should not be surprised. We know this enjoyment comes from the hands of a loving Creator who brought us into being with our best interests at heart. Hence, the Jerusalem Talmud states that in the life to come a person must give an account of every good thing he might have enjoyed in this life but did not (Kiddushin 4:12). In the rabbis' view, not to enjoy every legitimate pleasure was in essence to be an ingrate before the Master of the Universe." [24]

Perhaps overstated for effect, the essence of the thought is clear. Jewish affirmation of the physical world can also be seen in the positive view of physical work. In contrast to the Greek philosophers, who found manual labor beneath their dignity, the Hebrews found fulfillment in working with their hands.

It is significant to note that in Jesus' day it was expected that the rabbis would know a trade. The famous Rabbi Hillel was a woodcutter, and the equally famous Shammai, a carpenter. Paul, of course, was a tentmaker, and Jesus Himself was a carpenter. They were not ashamed of physical labor. In fact, quite the opposite. It was a shame for a father not to teach his son how to work with his hands. The Jewish Talmud says, "Just as a man is required to teach his son Torah [the Law], so is he required to teach him a trade" (Kiddushin 29a). It was felt that whoever did not teach his son the Law and a trade would bring him up to be a fool and a thief.

We should remember that physical labor itself is not the result of a curse upon man, for God instructed Adam to dress and keep the garden prior to the Fall (Genesis 2:15). It is also significant to note that the Hebrew word for work and worship is the same word: *avodah*. We will discuss this further, but first we need to see how Plato's dualistic views became mixed with Christian teaching, and what long-lasting negative effects this mixture has produced on Western Civilization.

## TRACING PLATO THROUGH THE CHURCH

How does this statement strike you? "Plato and Aristotle are among the greatest fathers of the Christian church. In spite of certain heretical doctrines, they might have been canonized in the Middle Ages, had they not happened to be born some centuries before the Christian era. Behind them both is Socrates, who perhaps would have waited longer to take his place in the company of the Saints with Joan of Arc."[25]

These words will provoke furrowed brows, if not audible moans and groans, from many Christians. The quote comes from a book published in 1972, entitled *Before and After Socrates*, written by Francis Cornford, an English historian who taught at Cambridge University. Unfortunately, Cornford's remarks are not historically unfounded, although the part about canonization of the Greeks might be stretching things a bit.

A merging of Plato's philosophy with Judaism actually did take place in Alexandria, Egypt, under the guiding hand of a Jewish philosopher by the name of Philo Judaeus, who is thought to have died in about A.D. 45. Alexandria was the chief center of Greek thought near the time of Christ. It was here that Philo developed a blend of Jewish thought and Greek philosophy sometimes referred to as Alexandrian Judaism. Philo interpreted Plato's forms as "thoughts of God," and believing Plato to be compatible with Judaism, he sought to merge the two.

As we have already seen, there were certain similarities between Plato and the Bible. But there are also certain similarities between a man and a monkey. Does this mean the two are compatible? Or does it imply the two are even related? We have seen what happens when people attempt to merge man and monkey into one. Remember the words of Peter Singer? The monkey does not become a man, but man becomes, in popular belief, an animal, thus losing his unique identity as an image-bearer of God. It's the same way with Plato and the Bible. If you try and merge the two, the true identity of God's Word is lost.

If the process had stopped with Philo's merging of Plato with Judaism, perhaps a different story would be told. But similar moves were made by certain church fathers, who held Greek philosophy in very high esteem. The tendency to incorporate popular philosophies of the day into Christianized forms is not just a present problem. It began very early.

Justin Martyr (c. 100-165), for example, was steeped in Platonic philosophy prior to his conversion to Christianity. After becoming a Christian, he incorporated Plato's thought into his teaching. He even referred to the Greek philosophers as Christians before Christ.[26]

Clement of Alexandria (c. 150-c. 215) said, "The same God that furnished both the Covenants was the giver of Greek philosophy to the Greeks."[27] He said God led the Greeks to Christ through philosophy even as He led the Jews to Him through the Law!

Origen, (c. 185-c. 232), called the Father of Christian Theology, was an influential Alexandrian philosopher, born and raised in that city, who is believed to have written several thousand books on various religious topics. He, too, incorporated Plato's ideas into Christian doctrine.[28]

Of course, this is not to say these men did not make very helpful contributions to the early church, especially as important defenders of the faith. But at the same time we must realize that, as with all people, not all of their thinking was without human tainting. Later, additional blending of Platonic philosophy with Christian teaching was fostered by Augustine, in the fourth century. Although in many respects Augustine was helpful to the church, and for this we must be grateful, he was influenced by Plotinus, a third-century Roman philosopher who is sometimes called the Father of Neo-platonism. Plotinus, like Plato, stressed the importance of meditation and contemplation on "the divine." Like Plato, Plotinus furthered a gulf between the spiritual realm and the material.

Augustine incorporated Plotinus' ideas into a Christian framework, making a great distinction between "contemplative life" and "active life." Prayer and meditation were "contemplative," while cleaning the kitchen floor or engaging in trade or business was "active." Contemplative life, to follow Augustinian thought, was of a higher order.

The blending of Plato's philosophy with the teachings of the church led to a religious dualism in which eternal concerns of the soul were set at odds with temporal concerns of the body. The "spiritual" life was a life detached from the material world as much as possible. Vows of poverty and celibacy were marks of serious spirituality. Even within marriage, Augustine's Platonic ideas led him to a very negative view of sexual intimacy, which he saw as shameful. The denial of physical pleasures, asceticism, was practiced by abstaining from foods, and sometimes even the self-infliction of physical pain. Seclusion from society was another form of self-denial, as were vows of silence.

From its earliest days, the church has been troubled by those who have taught that holiness is a matter of retreat, detachment, or withdrawal from this present life. The apostle Paul warned Timothy against the type of thinking which prohibited marriage or the enjoyment of foods which God created to be received with thanksgiving (1 Timothy 4:3-4).

A group called the Gnostics later taught that salvation was a matter of removing oneself from the world as much as possible so that a mystical union with God could be attained. Gnosticism was an early heresy which taught that the world was created by an evil deity who had rebelled against God. The world itself was an evil prison from which man needed to be rescued.

Even today there seems to be some confusion about what the "world" actually is, as mentioned in the Bible. The term is an important one to understand. It is used in Scripture several different ways. At times it refers to creation, such as in the biblical phrase "from the foundation of the world." At times it refers to the populated regions, such as when Paul wrote, "your faith is being proclaimed throughout the whole world."

But often the word has nothing to do with physical creation, geography or demographics. It is used to denote a way of life or a system of thought which is contrary to the will and ways of God. In this context, the "world" refers to a realm in which people act by their own rules, disregarding the lordship of Christ and the authority of God's Word. A person "of the world" is one whose source of approval is from earth (below) rather than from heaven (above), that is, from man or Satan, rather than from God.

The very first act of worldliness took place in the Garden of Eden when Adam and Eve ate fruit they were told not to eat. They acted by the authority of this world – their own – and disregarded God's. But is eating fruit a worldly act in and of itself? Of course not. It all depends upon the context. In the case of Adam and Eve, eating this particular fruit was a worldly act, because it violated the authority from above. But we cannot conclude from this incident that fruit is bad, or that eating it is sinful. The determining factor of worldliness is not found in the fruit itself, or the act of eating it, but rather in disregarding the revealed will of God.

Christians, of all people, cannot afford to confuse God's good creation with man's bad choices. To do so leads to disdain for that which God meant for us to partake of with thanksgiving and joy. The Hebrew model of holiness does not mean that a person detaches himself from the physical world or legitimate pleasures found in it. It does not mean that a man suppresses his God-given humanity by disclaiming or denying physical pleasure in an effort to distance himself from the material world. Holiness does mean, however, that a person learns to control his passions instead of being controlled by them, submitting to God's good authority throughout every aspect of creation. It means that a person freely partakes of the good things of life within the boundaries of God's loving borders. It means a disciplined life, to be sure, but an abundant life within prescribed borders.

The Christian must not view the physical body as something evil, or a prison from which to be rescued, but rather as a temple indwelt by God Himself. He wants to employ it for His purposes in the world, while we are still here. It would be nice to think that the problem of religious dualism in Christian practice is a thing of the past, but such is not the case. The shadow of Plato is a hard thing for the church to dispel. The blending of Greek thinking with the early teachings of the church planted seeds for movements hundreds of years later which stressed the eternal side of life and denounced the temporal to such a degree that Christians retreated from active roles in such "worldly" pursuits as politics, the arts, and science, withdrawing from the mainstream of life itself.

But denial of the physical world, or detachment from it, runs counter to responsible stewardship over it. Our unique calling as humans is not to detach ourselves from the material, temporal world, but to interact with it according to the will and ways of God, doing His will on earth as it is in heaven, being in the world but not of it, occupying until He comes.

Politics, then, is not a worldly occupation in and of itself. It only becomes so when people who practice it do so in a manner which violates the revealed Word of God, and crosses over the moral borders provided by our Creator. The same can be said of all legitimate professions and endeavors.

Yet, even today, Christian "spirituality" is often focused on the contemplative life of the inner experience of the soul, indirectly deemphasizing the value of active roles for Christians in the world of temporal concerns. It is still commonly held that a young man or woman who desires to truly serve God in this life will do so by becoming a pastor or missionary. Such work is often referred to as "fulltime Christian service," while other vocations are simply something less. To think this way is distinctly unbiblical, and has been devastating to the effectiveness of Christians in bringing wholeness and health to life in the here and now.

We said that the shadow of Plato is a hard thing for the church to dispel. This is true, but the shadow of Plato can be dispelled, with a little change of thinking, which we will talk about shortly. But before we do, a few words need to be said about Aristotle, and the lasting effect he, too, has had upon the West.

## THE INFLUENCE OF ARISTOTLE ON WESTERN CIVILIZATION

When it came to influencing Western thought, Aristotle's ideas worked like a drug store "time release capsule." His writings had no effect on Western thinking for hundreds of years, until in the twelfth century they began to have an effect, as seeds were sown which set in motion a movement of thought which has not slowed down yet.

Aristotle was a student of Plato, but his interests were much more in the here-and-now world of physical matter. He is sometimes called the Father of the Scientific Method, and was the first to classify the physical world into specific fields of biology, zoology, and physics. He is also known as the founder of logic. His work covered a very wide range, including ethics, politics, and metaphysics.

Unlike Plato, his writings were not incorporated into the thinking of the early church. But they were nurtured and further developed by the Moslems via Arabic translations, which eventually found their way into Spain. In the eleventh century this information, which included not only Greek but Arabic math and science, became known to the church largely by way of Latin translations by Jewish scholars.

Here was a vast body of knowledge not previously encountered by the church. In education, ever since the start of European universities, the Queen of the Sciences had been theology. But with the coming of Aristotle, there emerged a new interest in the physical world. Along with this information came the realization that Aristotle accumulated his wealth of knowledge apart from any assistance from the church or the Bible, using human logic, reason, and observation as his guide. Here the church was not an authority. This was no minor matter, for at this time the church enjoyed a position of unchallenged power and authority, dominating European thought and culture.

The response of the church was varied. Some accepted Aristotle's reason-based approach to life wholly and willingly. The twelfth-century scholar Peter Abelard went so far as to imply that whatever could not be proven true through logic was considered false.

We previously discussed the fact that reason in itself is not something negative. It is a positive thing, a part of God's likeness in man which separates us from the animals. But when one leans upon reason solely and independently of revelation, and makes reason the final judge of truth, a very strange thing begins to happen: reason reasons out revelation altogether. This is what slowly took place on the European stage between the 1200s and the 1700s.

In the 1200s, Thomas Aquinas sought to accommodate the work of Aristotle with the church and make room for both to coexist under the blessing of church authority. His work, knows as Thomistic Scholasticism, brought together reason-based and revelation-based thinking into a new and acceptable whole. He did this by dividing life into two distinct realms: the realm of Nature and the realm of Grace. In the lower realm of Nature, which included science, logic, and things having to do with the natural, temporal world, man's intellect and independent reason operated quite well on its own. Reason was seen as a reliable guide to truth in this realm. Revelation, on the other hand, was necessary for understanding the upper realm of Grace, which included such things as theology, prayer, worship, God, angels, and things pertaining to the eternal, supernatural world.

### GRACE
*God, angels, prayer, worship – matters having to do with the supernatural, eternal, spiritual realm.*

### NATURE
*Science, logic, economics, etc. – matters having to do with the natural, temporal, material realm.*

Aquinas did not intend for the realm of Grace to be in opposition to Nature, or vice versa. He taught that the realm of Nature must be subjected to the authority of the church. But by simply placing the material world in a category of its own, even though initially connected to the realm of Grace, over time the distinction became so great in people's minds that the connection disappeared altogether.

As the serious study of the world of the here-and-now went its own independent way, guided by the light of human reason alone, the voice of the church was relegated to a narrow sphere of life known as "religion." By the 1700s the rift was firmly in place, at least in Europe, as the light of independent reason in opposition to all supernatural religion became the driving force of what historians call the "Enlightenment." The term, of course, contrasts with the preceding era labeled the "Dark Ages." The new light of the age was human reason, not divine revelation.

This is the mark of modernism, where there is a blatant disregard for revelation and high regard for reason, where Nature (capital N) is the sole, impersonal, "creative guiding intelligence" of the universe; where the Word of God is considered as relevant as the proclamations of Zeus, where human reason is the sole measurement of ethics, morality, and freedom. Although the advent of postmodernism in the second half of the twentieth century brought with it a reaction to such an extreme elevation of reason, the stronghold of human reason over divine revelation is as powerful as ever.

Because the Judeo-Christian roots of our American culture are as strong as they are, we are presently in the throes of a great ideological wrestling match. We have in our society a fairly large number of people who still hold to biblical assumptions about life, much to the displeasure of others who would like to see these "remnants of the Dark Ages" extinguished once and for all, not only from our public schools and civil government, but from our socially accepted views of family and morality.

The battle has been intense in recent years. There has been a prolific increase of people in our culture who no longer take biblical assumptions for granted. Leadership in our society is being increasingly held by people whose public school experience did not include the reading of Scripture, or the posting of the Ten Commandments on the wall, but did include a very Greek approach to morality which led people to decide for themselves what is right or wrong.

Prior to the 1960s, most Americans, even those who did not claim to be Christians, held to a biblical framework of morality. They did this whether they knew where it came from or not. Back then it was not uncommon for people to refer to the United States as a "Christian nation," because its laws were openly based upon the Bible, and the words of Jesus Christ were honored and recognized as authoritative.

But today it is a different story. Increasingly, every man is doing what is right in his own eyes, regardless of what Scripture has to say. As one pastor put it, we are living in a time "when right has become wrong, wrong has become right, and it is wrong to say wrong is wrong." [29]

The question naturally comes, then, if things have changed so rapidly in our culture in the past fifty years, what will our culture be like in another generation, should God grant us the time? Will the next generation live in a society where biblical assumptions are alive and well, as they once were in America, or will these ancient foundation stones be replaced with other ancient ideas?

This book was written with the hope of the former, not the latter. It was written for the purpose of helping people to understand the root issues, and to help them see how far the rising tide of ancient pagan thinking has flooded the land – and where the current is rapidly taking us. It was also written with the thought in mind of letting people know what can be done to repair the dikes.

By God's enabling, much can be done to reverse the trend. Certainly within the context of individual families a standard of biblical thought and practice can be restored, as Christian parents do their part to nurture the next generation, as we have previously discussed. For parents, there is no greater calling or ministry than this. As the family goes, so goes the nation. While many people may not have an opportunity to be a direct influence in the arenas of law, civil government, education, or the arts, every parent will have an opportunity to influence their own home, and thus many generations to follow.

Yet outside the home, many Christians will indeed have opportunities to be of significant influence. It is with the hope also that they will be encouraged to do so that this book was written. An important step in regaining Christian influence in our culture is to reassess our own assumptions, to be sure they are biblically sound. Are we really thinking biblically about our work, our schools and our civil responsibilities? The remainder of this book will examine these issues in particular. But first, we must address the problem of religious dualism in our everyday thought, which has hindered Christians from fully appreciating their role in the world of the here-and-now.

## OVERCOMING DUALISM

A person looks at two buildings, a cathedral and a skyscraper, classifying one as a sacred place of worship and the other as a secular place of business; a person reads two books, the Bible and *Black Beauty*, regarding the one as a sacred book and the other as a secular book; a violinist plays two pieces, *How Great Thou Art* and Beethoven's Sonata in C Minor, calling the one a sacred piece, and the other a secular piece; a person studies two paintings, one of The Last Supper and the other of an elderly farmer standing with his wife at his right side and a pitchfork at his left, categorizing the one as sacred art and the other as secular; a factory worker listens to a pastor preach on Sunday morning, thinking the pastor's work is a sacred task, while viewing his own work as a secular job.

These are common examples of contrived religious dualism, which are the result of the fabricated mixture of Greek philosophy with the teachings of the church. In an unfortunate way, Plato's elevating of metaphysical ideals and relative devaluing of the physical world, incorporated into the teachings of the church by early theologians, has been a part of Western thought for hundreds of years, both inside and outside of the church.

It is generally accepted that life can, and should, be divided into two major categories: the "sacred" and the "secular," even though neither word can be found in the Bible. A "sacred" place is where we worship God, a "secular" place is where we do our work. The "sacred" division of life has to do with things associated with the church, while the "secular" has to do with things associated with matters outside of the church. The "sacred" things of life are clearly connected with God, while in the "secular world" there is no direct connection, or at least the connection is not really relevant.

But is there such a world? Is there any part of life not connected with God in a very direct and significant way? Is there any aspect of life in which God is not relevant? Let's think about the cathedral and the skyscraper for a moment. How are the elements of both buildings held together? Does the skyscraper somehow exist independently of God? No. By Him all things consist (Col. 1:16-17). Who gave the architects the ability to design these structures, and the construction crew the ability to put the pieces together? Christians or not, it is only because man was made in the likeness of God, with the ability to design and create, that such buildings are even possible. A skyscraper is a magnificent tribute to God, whether those who made it realize it or not. To think God could make such a creation as man, with the ability to build a skyscraper, is awe-inspiring.

As if this were not enough, consider: Who owns the skyscraper? "The earth is the Lord's, and all it contains" (Ps. 24:1, NAS). What is "secular" about property which belongs to God? And in addition to all this, if there is a Christian inside that building who is doing his or her job "heartily as unto the Lord" (Col. 3:23), the skyscraper is in fact a place of worship. As mentioned previously, the Hebrew word for work and worship are the same: *avodah*. This gives us a hint to the Hebrew view of the unity and wholeness of life under God, in which one's work is as much an expression of response to Him as one's prayer.

Let's think about art for a moment. The fact that a person can create a painting on canvas is another great tribute to the Lord, whether the artist knows Him or not. Truly beautiful art can't help but glorify God, even if the artist is an atheist, and the subject matter has nothing to do with religion. Whether it is a painting of The Last Supper of Jesus, or a Norman Rockwell painting of the family home for supper, the fact that people can create such things and other people can see and appreciate them is amazing. Light waves created and sustained by God reflect the full spectrum of color placed in paint on a flat canvas by human hands, registering images upon the viewer's brain, creating emotions or a sense of wonder. Is any of this possible apart from God? And again, if the artist does his or her painting as unto the Lord, in a manner that does not dishonor Him, the act itself is worship, whether the subject matter is a biblical scene or not.

Similar comments could be made about all forms of art, including music and literature. As for the story of *Black Beauty*, neither the color black, nor beauty, nor horses are "secular." Furthermore, if an author writes as unto the Lord, with content that does not dishonor Him or His Word, he or she does not have to write a sermon or present a Christian moral in order to glorify God through the molding of words. The same can be said for molding the sound of music.

We could go on with more examples, but the point is simply this: The "sacred/secular" dualism is not legitimate. It confuses the real issues, and misleads people into thinking certain aspects of life pertain to God, while others do not. Yet, life cannot be divided up like this. God is the God of the spiritual as well as the material, the God of the eternal as well as the temporal. He is just as relevant to the things of time as He is to the things of eternity, and as relevant to the things of church as He is to things outside of church.

It isn't really possible to detach God from any sphere of reality, try as we might. While the word "secular" may be used to identify a sphere of life in which God is ignored, it cannot be used to identify a sphere of life in which God is irrelevant. Such a "secular" world does not exist, except in the imaginations of people who have heard it talked about so long they think it is really there.

The question now comes, if the sacred/secular dualism is not a legitimate way of viewing life, then how should we think about life? If there is no "secular" world, then does this mean everything is "sacred"? What about things that are obviously contrary to the will of God, or violate His Word? What about a business that is out of line with His moral precepts?

These are good questions. Finding the answers require us to look at life from a much different perspective than we may be accustomed to. It means viewing the world through a different window, seeing things more like Abraham, and less like Plato. It means viewing life through a vertical distinction, rather than a horizontal one.

What does that mean? Well, let's go back to Plato's view of the world for just a moment. We can diagram his worldview by forming a circle, representing the whole of reality. The solid line drawn horizontally across the middle represents a division into two levels, an upper and a lower level.

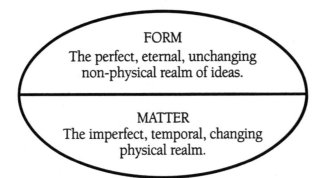

FORM
The perfect, eternal, unchanging
non-physical realm of ideas.

MATTER
The imperfect, temporal, changing
physical realm.

In terms of Plato's metaphysical idealism, the upper has to do with the eternal, unchanging, and perfect world of ideals, while the lower level has to do with the temporal, changing, and imperfect world of physical matter. This idea, later adapted and incorporated into the thinking of the church, resulted in a sacred/secular view of the world.

In the diagram below, we see reality divided into an upper level of "sacred" concerns pertaining to the spiritual, eternal, and unchanging realm of God in heaven, and a lower level of "secular" concerns pertaining to the physical, temporal, and changing realm of man on earth. The upper level has to do with things like prayer, meditation, Bible study, singing of hymns, preaching, evangelism, Sunday services, and other so-called "religious" activities.

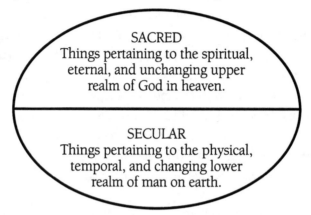

In the lower level would be such things as washing the dishes, Monday through Friday employment, computer technology, science, sports, entertainment, and other so-called "secular" activities. If we were to diagram a perspective that would come closer to a biblical view of life, it would look something more like this:

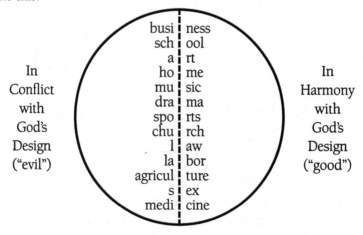

Here, rather than a horizontal solid line dividing reality into upper and lower divisions, we see a broken line running vertically through all reality. The broken line signifies the fact that any particular aspect of life may shift from one side of the line to the other, depending on certain factors, as described below.

Since we have previously mentioned the area of politics, or civil government, we'll start there. As we said earlier, politics, in and of itself, is not a "worldly" endeavor, it only becomes so when people who practice it do so in a manner which violates the guidelines of God's Word. We cannot say that political activity is a "secular" endeavor, existing in a contrived compartment of "non-sacred" life, functioning by its own set of guidelines, independent from God's thoughts on the matter of civil government and human relations. We can, however, say that political activity which is in harmony with God's Word is good, while political activity which is in conflict with God's Word is corrupt.

Now here is the basic assumption we are dealing with: God is not just relevant to the so-called "sacred" things of life, but to all things under His authority, and since there is nothing which stands outside of His authority, He is as relevant to what goes on in civil government as He is to the way business functions, to the way family members relate to one another, to the way one's personal ethics are ordered, to the way a local church functions. In short, He is Lord of all, and no less relevant to one area of human endeavor than another, and certainly no less relevant to what goes on outside the church than He is to what goes on inside the church.

For the Hebrew, life and worship were inseparable. For them, there were no sacred moments interspersed among secular pursuits. Although there were certainly moments in which the focus of attention was directed toward God in special ways, this did not imply that when one returned home to plow his field or tend his sheep that this other activity was less of an act of response to God.

This was in contrast to the Greek, whose religious focus was upon ritual, such as chants, and food offerings to gods, etc., which varied according to family tradition. It was the ritual that was strictly adhered to, and the issue of correct ritual received more emphasis than conduct, a matter in which the gods themselves were not exactly exemplary.

The Greek did not look to any objective Word of God in such issues as interpersonal relationships or moral standards. While Greek religion required adherence to ritual, it did not require a commitment to any particular way of life. So a Greek could be a religious person and yet live according to whatever personal creed or human philosophy he chose, providing it did not violate the laws of the city-state. For them, observing sacred ceremonies was one matter, while the rest of life was quite another, with religion playing a part in ancient Greece, but remaining just that – a part. But for the Hebrew, worship was a way of life, and God was equally relevant to every endeavor.

It is to be the same for us today. No matter in which sphere of life we find ourselves, as we order our ways in accordance with God or in discordance with Him, the activity we engage in may be pulled to one side of the vertical line or the other, depending on the choices we make and the motives of our hearts. The biblical dualism in life, then, is not between "sacred" and "secular," in contrived upper and lower levels of life, but rather between that which is in harmony with God's design or in conflict with it, that is, between good and evil, no matter in what sphere of life or endeavor it takes place.

The question is, will the government of the state function in accordance with the higher laws of God, or in opposition to them? Will businessmen operate by biblical ethics or be swayed by the lure of a quick buck? Will our use of medicine honor God or dishonor Him? Will our home life be in line with God's design for the family, or will it be something which operates according to the so-called wisdom of this world?

As we align our ways with God's ways, be it in our home lives, our business lives, or our entertainment lives, any legitimate activity has the potential to be beautiful, good, pleasing to God, and truly fulfilling. If we choose to reject God's guidelines, we will find that no matter in what sphere of life we function, the result distorts what God has created and is truly unfulfilling.

The body is not intrinsically "bad" while the soul is intrinsically "good." Both are equal parts of God's good creation, but each, as a result of the Fall, may actively participate in good or evil, depending on one's choice to act in harmony with God's Word or contrary to it. Man's sexuality, for instance, is a part of God's good creation. Experienced within the guidelines of His design, it is a beautiful thing. Sexual perversion, on the other hand, is a matter of sexual practice contrary to His design.

Good and evil are possibilities in any arena of life. Good government, then, is government in harmony with God's guidelines, whether at the state level, in the church, or in the home. Corrupt government is that which disregards God's

Word, and functions contrary to it. Civil, church, and family authorities are equally God-ordained and equally obligated to the Higher Authority from Whom all authority originates.

As a result of the Fall and the entrance of sin into the world, God's good creation has indeed suffered. It has been abused, violated, twisted, and perverted by men. But we must constantly come back to the truth that in spite of its present condition, the earth and all it contains still belongs to God. He has not abandoned it. The whole sphere of life, even if it exists in its present form for only a short season, must be viewed as having its original created goodness, its distortions through the Fall, and its redeemed purpose.

Life takes on a new and challenging meaning when viewed through the window we're talking about here. Our call to responsible stewardship and cultivation of creation must be seen as a valued task fulfilled under God in the here and now. While sin's entrance into the world has resulted in death, separation from God, pain and suffering, we must not conclude that the earth and its contents are worthless, only to be discarded by God as good for nothing but final judgment. It is not a matter of polishing brass on a sinking ship, but of affirming life as God's good creation, and entering into our purpose as His image-bearing stewards while we are here.

**CHAPTER FIVE SUMMARY: KEY PEOPLE, PLACES AND CONCEPTS**

Homer (c. 800 B.C.)

*Iliad* and *Odyssey*

Xenophanes (c. 560-c. 478 B.C.)

Protagoras of Abdera (c. 485-410 B.C.)

The Sophists

Socrates (c. 470-399)

Plato (427-347 B.C.)

Philo Judaeus (c. 13 B.C.-c. A.D.45)

Alexandria, Egypt

Justin Martyr (c. 100-c. 165)

Clement of Alexandria (c. 150-c. 215)

Augustine (354-430)

Plotinus (205-270)

Thomas Aquinas (1225-1274)

Worldview

Dabhar
The three meanings of the word "world" in the Bible
Dualism
Idealism
Unchanging universals versus changing particulars
Form and matter
Alexandrian Judaism
Platonic Christianity
Contemplative life versus active life
Sacred versus secular
Gnosticism
The Hebrew view of holiness
Nature versus grace
Thomastic Scholasticism
The Enlightenment

## For Further Thought and Discussion

1. Consider examples of how assumptions cause different people to view the same things in vastly different ways. Take an item from the daily news and discuss how that item might be interpreted from the perspective of an evolutionist, a creationist, a moral relativist, a moral absolutist, an individualist, a collectivist, a reason-based thinker, and/or a revelation-based thinker.

2. How did the guiding light of Greek philosophy also cause it to degenerate?

3. "The most effective lies are those which come as close to the truth as possible." Give examples from philosophy and religion. How does this apply to Platonic Christianity?

4. "Religion itself can be one of the most worldly of all endeavors." Explain.

5. Summarize the differences between Plato and Aristotle.

# Chapter Six

# What Are the Borders
# of the Kingdom of God?

D escribing the kingdom of God is like the blind men describing an elephant. One man holds its tail, and says it's like a rope. Another man touches its leg, and decides it's like a tree. Another feels its side, and says it's like a wall. If you had never seen an elephant, and you heard the blind men's reports, you might be confused unless you realized the elephant is really like "all of the above," at one point or another, depending on where you put your focus.

In this chapter we will deal with the kingdom of God in its broadest sense. A common dictionary definition of the word kingdom reads: "A country ruled by a king or queen." In the broadest sense of the word, God's kingdom is that domain over which He is King. Taken in this context, then, the kingdom of God is as broad as creation is wide, for there is no realm which exists independently of God's sovereign rule and authority, either in heaven or on earth.

There is no place we can go to remove ourselves from God's dominion. As King David put it, "The Lord has established His throne in heaven, and His kingdom rules over all" (Psalm 103:19). This is the kingdom of God at large. It has no borders whatsoever. David knew he could not escape it even if he went to the farthest reaches of the planet.

Our Lord is Lord of heaven and Lord of earth, even though not everybody on earth knows or acknowledges Him as such. Whether a person recognizes it or not, Jesus is still the King of all kings, and the Lord of all lords. Human disregard for God does not invalidate His authority over each and every one of us, Christian or not. While not everyone on earth is a son or daughter of the kingdom of God, they are still living in God's kingdom whether they realize it or not.

"The earth is the Lord's and all it contains, the world, and those who dwell in it" (Psalm 24:1). By virtue of God's creating and sustaining of the whole earth, all its contents are His. Though human beings may deny His very existence, or even curse Him daily, He still sustains their very breath. He not only owns the cattle on a thousand hills, but the hills themselves are His, along with everything that walks on them, flies over them, or digs under them, including man, redeemed or not. By creation, all men are His handiwork. Though not all are His by the second birth, they are all His by the first.

Everything that man puts his hand to belongs to God. While enjoying a meal at a fine restaurant it is important to realize that not only the food comes from Him, but the plate one eats from, the table one sits at, as well as the wallpaper and the candles. It doesn't matter whether the owner realizes it or not, the whole restaurant belongs to God.

Yet, even though it all belongs to God, ever since the first temptation of man, the earth and all it contains have been contested ground. There is an enemy who lays claim to that which is God's. He is the great usurper of God's authority, an infiltrating squatter on God's land, and a contrary voice within the borders of God's kingdom at large, having established a rebel kingdom of his own inside the true King's territory.

This enemy, Satan, has sought since the beginning of man's history to draw men away from the Creator, trying his utmost to tear down and destroy all that is God's and to claim it for his own. He is called in Scripture the one who "deceives the whole world" (Revelation 12:9), and He has done such an effective job that many Christians have been duped into believing the earth indeed is his. But in reality the devil has never created anything in his life. He has only twisted and perverted that which God has made.

Because of the Fall, man now lives in an abnormal and distorted world. Things are not the way God originally made them to be. God's good creation has been abused, misused, and warped. As a result of man's disregard of the King and His authority, the earth and all it contains has suffered since the day of the first sin. People get sick and die. Wars cripple and kill. Children sometimes starve to death. These are the harsh realities of a fallen world. Yet, it is God's very creation that suffers.

Man lives in a world of two kingdoms at war. One realm is made up of those who are of God, and the other is made up of those who are of this world. It is those who are of this world who lie under the power of the evil one. For Satan, too, is very much a ruler on planet earth, at least for a season. Yet, he is the ruler of this world system (John 12:31; 16:11; 2 Corinthians 4:3-4), and his ways are from below – not from above.

While one kingdom is of heaven and the other is of this world, they are both simultaneously in (or, on) the earth today. For the time being, both wheat and tares are growing in the same field. Jesus spoke plainly about this mystery in one of the parables of Matthew 13. Here He told of a man who sowed good seed in his field, but an enemy came and sowed weeds among the wheat. Jesus' disciples later asked for an explanation of the story, which is recorded in verses 37-43:

And He answered and said, "The one who sows the good seed is the Son of Man, and the field is the world; and as for the good seed, these are the sons of the kingdom; and the tares are the sons of the evil one; and the enemy who sowed them is the devil, and the harvest is the end of the age; and the reapers are angels.

Therefore just as the tares are gathered up and burned with fire, so shall it be at the end of the age. The Son of Man will send forth His angels, and they will gather out of His kingdom all stumbling blocks and those who commit lawlessness, and will cast them into the furnace of fire; in that place there shall be weeping and gnashing of teeth. Then the righteous will shine forth as the sun in the kingdom of their Father. He who has ears, let him hear." (NAS)

Notice the stumbling blocks and lawless ones, sons of the evil one, are gathered out of God's kingdom at the end of the age. Here we see those who are of the enemy living in God's kingdom. Until the time of harvest, both good seed and bad are growing in God's field, which is the created world (earth) itself. In spite of the fact that an enemy has come and sowed bad seed, God's kingdom is as still as broad as the world is wide. Yet, while many Christians sing the hymn *This Is My Father's World* on Sunday morning, when they look around on Monday it does not seem as if it is really true. They see so many weeds they lose sight of the fact the field itself is God's.

Feeling outnumbered and overwhelmed, many Christians retreat and focus attention upon an inner world of personal "spirituality," leaving the "other" world for the enemy to occupy. Or they focus their attention on the church, limiting the borders of God's kingdom to this one institution. This is a serious case of nearsightedness, for the kingdom of God extends far beyond the jurisdiction of the church.

Unfortunately, because of dualistic, sacred/secular thinking among Christians, a truly effective application of biblical thought and practice to the whole of our culture "out there" has been short-circuited. Christians have become their own worst enemies, it seems, having spiritualized themselves right out of the ball game and on to the bench.

In placing spiritual concerns or activities of the church in a contrived upper sphere, religious dualism by default places everything else in a lower sphere. In doing this, a hierarchy of values is created whereby the church and church-related activity are at the top, while activities not specifically church-related are second-rate, less relevant to what really matters in life, or simply not as pleasing to God.

As a consequence, sincere Christians in so-called secular occupations who desire to do "the Lord's work" often labor under some degree of discontent. Seeing their work itself as a spiritual activity of worth or an act of worship to God is difficult. After all, if one's spirituality is measured in terms of devotion to things of God which are part of a contrived upper level of spirituality, then there is no getting around the idea that one's involvement within a perceived lower sphere of life is certainly less spiritual, if spiritual at all. Such unfortunate thinking fails to take into consideration that the things of God fill the "lower" and "upper" levels (if you will) with equal force.

Of course, the health and well-being of the local church is certainly vital to each and every community. We must have strong churches in the land. But vital, too, is the health and well-being of the city council, as well as local businesses, farms, homes, and schools. As Christian farmers, businessmen, civil servants, parents, and educators, we can and should be involved in doing "the Lord's work" no matter where we are planted in the kingdom of God at large, doing our work heartily as unto the Lord, for His glory in all the earth. This is true worship at work.

Our great challenge, then, is to learn to "think Christianly" about civil government, economics, law, medicine, science, the media, and the arts. We need judges who will judge Christianly, economists who will manage money Christianly, teachers who will teach Christianly, governors who will govern Christianly, plumbers who will plumb Christianly, and parents who will parent Christianly. We can no longer afford to privatize our Christianity or limit our understanding of God's kingdom to the church or to the world beyond the grave. This is not a new and strange doctrine. Listen to the words of A.A. Hodge, the nineteenth century theologian who taught at Princeton:

[A Christian] has no right to separate his life into two realms, and acknowledge different moral codes in each respectively – to say the Bible is a good rule for Sunday, but this is a week-day question; or the Scriptures are the right rule in matters of religion, but this is a question of business or of politics. God reigns over all everywhere. His will is the supreme law in all relations and actions. His inspired Word, loyally read, will inform us of His will in every relation and act of life, secular as well as religious; and the man is a traitor who refuses to walk therein with scrupulous care. The kingdom of God includes all sides of human life, and it is a kingdom of absolute righteousness. You are either a loyal subject or a traitor. When the King comes, how will he find you doing? [30]

In limiting our understanding of the kingdom of God to a privatized world of personal spirituality or the organized world of the church, Christians have retreated from stewardship over very large portions of reality. In abdicating responsibility throughout God's kingdom at large, Christians have created a cultural vacuum of labor, influence, and leadership which the ungodly have come in to fill. The fact of the matter is, someone is going to exercise rulership in the earth. If not the godly, then the ungodly. If the righteous retreat completely, they have no reason to be surprised when they wake up one day to find their inheritance (the earth) usurped by those who do not know God.

Historically, the unfortunate results of limiting the kingdom of God to the church can be seen in what happened at the end of the Middle Ages as the church lost its position of prominence in European culture. It seems the kingdom of God had become, in the minds of many, equated with the kingdom of church. And as the borders of the church's authority shrank, the perceived sphere of God's kingdom and His right to speak shrank right along with it.

This problem could only have happened in a worldview with a horizontal sacred/secular split. Because of the contrived horizontal split between "sacred" and "secular" worlds, as the so-called secular world grew in prominence it squeezed the so-called sacred world into a corner of life called "religion," imprisoned it there, and now vigilantly stands guard to make sure it doesn't escape. As a result of this development, God's authority in today's world has been relegated to a narrow sphere of life called "religion." So it is today that the Bible is seen as relevant to Sunday sermons and seminary studies, but its authority in the arena of economics, law, and sociology is virtually ignored by contemporary men and women.

We often hear today that religion is a "private matter," a "personal thing," applicable only to one's private life, or to what goes on in church, and certainly not to matters of employment, government, or business. The Bible's words, it is believed, have no relevancy to society as a whole. Outside the church or one's personal life, Scripture is simply not acceptable.

An example of this assumption can be seen in the case of Dr. Kenneth Olson, a Phoenix, Arizona Christian psychologist, whose encounter with the privatization of Christianity and the sacred/secular dualism of contemporary thought led to a revocation of his license to practice:

[A] child was placed in foster care because his parents, who were Satanists, had physically and sexually abused him. The foster parents put the child in psychiatric care at the Arizona State Hospital after he became violent and destructive. When the hospital's treatment was unsuccessful, the foster mother took the boy, with permission from the hospital and ADES [Arizona Department of Economic Security], to see Dr. Olson. At the first session, the child fell asleep, and Dr. Olson prayed that demonic spirits would be removed from him. After 15 minutes of prayer, the boy awoke, became angry and crawled under a table. Dr. Olson continued to pray, and within minutes the child regained a sweet and loving disposition. The child did not manifest the violent behavior again. His progress was so remarkable that he was soon discharged from the Arizona State Hospital and returned to the foster home. Dr. Olson continued weekly outpatient therapy for five months.

In September 1992, however, two ADES employees filed a complaint with the ABPE [Arizona Board of Psychologists Examiners] alleging that Dr. Olson was unable to separate his work as a psychologist from that of a religious minister. On Oct. 18, 1993, Dr. Olson's license to practice was revoked by the Board. The Rutherford Institute has filed suit.[31]

Prevalent today is the grand assumption that the Creator is simply not relevant to the entire spectrum of life. Period. The notion that God has any say in matters beyond the personal, private realm of Bible-believing individuals is politically incorrect. This way of thinking is reflected in those who tell us it is all right to be "personally opposed" to killing pre-born children in the womb, but you "can't legislate morality." It's O.K. to be religious, they may tell us, "but please go to church to do it, or keep it personal." In essence, what they are saying is, "God's authority may apply to His kingdom, but that kingdom doesn't go beyond the church's parking lot or your back fence."

With regard to the slogan, "You can't legislate morality," it is certainly true if one means to say people cannot be forced by legislation to be moral. But while we can't legislate morality in this sense, we certainly can legislate consequences for immorality. We can, and we must, legislate deterrents to behavior that is immoral, for the good of society. This is what legislation is for. [32]

In the minds of many today, God's Word regarding what is moral or immoral has not even a general relevancy to public policy in America, even though the founding fathers would be horrified if they knew we had abandoned the guidelines of Scripture as a basis of morality and law in everyday life and government. It was accepted among early Americans that although the government of the state should not be mixed with the government of the church, or vice versa, an adherence to the basic precepts of Scripture and principles of Christianity in civil affairs was vital to the ongoing success of our republic. Since this may be a surprise to many Americans today, including Christians, it is worth a closer look.

### CHRISTIAN PRINCIPLE, CIVIL GOVERNMENT, AND EARLY AMERICA

In 1974, two political scientists from the University of Houston, Donald Lutz and Charles Hyneman, set out to read virtually all the political writings of Americans published between 1760 and 1805. This included all books, pamphlets, newspaper articles, and monographs on the subject of civil government written for the general public of that day. They wanted to find out which European thinkers had most influenced the ideas of America's founders during the time known as the "founding era," when the early state and national constitutions were framed. The researchers felt that by identifying who the founders quoted in their writings, they would discover whose ideas these men were being most influenced by.

Starting with 15,000 writings, and narrowing it down to some 2,200 writings which dealt specifically with political content, Lutz and Hyneman identified 3,154 quotes or references from other sources. About ten years after they started the project, their findings were published in *The American Political Science Review.* What they discovered was, the single source most often quoted by the founders of America was not European at all, but Middle Eastern: the Bible. In fact, 34 percent of all quotes were from this one source! [33]

Now, in a day when we've been told it's unconstitutional to instruct from the Bible in a public classroom, or to post the Ten Commandments on a public schoolroom wall, or to even put up a nativity scene in front of a U.S. post office, it's rather amazing to know that the very men who founded American government in the first place turned to the Bible so often for direction and support for their ideas.

But were the principles of Christianity actually mixed with civil government in America? Of course they were! The history of America clearly demonstrates this. Christianity was freely and openly mixed with civil affairs in this nation for 160 years. From 1787, when the Constitution was first formed, until 1947, when the Supreme Court first suggested otherwise. In fact, the idea of not mixing Christianity with civil affairs would have been strongly objected to by most of the founding fathers.

In the 1830s, the French historian Alexis de Tocqueville came to examine America. He wrote a book about what he discovered, entitled, *Democracy in America.* The following excerpts will give you a flavor for the day, some fifty years after the framing of the Constitution, from the perspective of an outside observer:

From the earliest settlement of the emigrants, politics and religion contracted an alliance which has never been dissolved. [p. 281]... I do not know whether all the Americans have a sincere faith in their religion; for who can search the human heart? But I am certain that they hold it to be indispensable to the maintenance of republican institutions. This opinion is not peculiar to a class of citizens or to a party, but it belongs to the whole nation, and to every rank of society. [p. 286-287]... The Americans combine the notions of Christianity and of liberty so intimately in their minds, that it is impossible to make them conceive the one without the other. [p. 287]... Upon my arrival in the United States, the religious aspect of the country was the first thing that struck my attention; and the longer I stayed there, the more did I perceive the great political consequences resulting from this state of things, to which I was unaccustomed. In France I had almost always seen the spirit of religion and the spirit of freedom pursuing courses diametrically opposed to each other; but in America I found that they were intimately united, and that they reigned in common over the same country. [p. 289] America is still the place where the Christian religion has kept the greatest real power over men's souls; and nothing better demonstrates how useful and natural it is to man, since the country where it now has the widest sway is both the most enlightened and the freest... [p. 291] [34]

So much for not mixing Christianity with politics! George Washington, sometimes called the Father of our Country, said in his "Farewell Address" that political prosperity was based upon two "indispensable supports," namely, religion and morality: "Of all the dispositions and habits which lead to political prosperity, religion and morality are indispensable supports. In vain would that man claim the tribute of patriotism, who should labor to subvert these great pillars." [35]

John Adams spoke plainly when he declared that: "...we have no government armed with power capable of contending with human passions unbridled by morality and religion. Our Constitution was made only for a moral and religious people. It is wholly inadequate to the government of any other." [36]

Do you think the religion these men had in mind was anything other than Christianity? Do you think the morality they spoke of was anything other than the morality defined by the Bible? Hardly! One would have to rewrite the history of this nation to keep from arriving at any other than this conclusion.

Consider these words by Woodrow Wilson on the subject:

We know that there is a standard set for us in the heavens, a standard revealed to us in this book [the Bible] which is the fixed and eternal standard by which we judge ourselves... We do not judge progress by material standards. America is not ahead of other nations of the world because she is rich. Nothing makes America great except her thoughts, except her ideals, except her acceptance of those standards of judgment which are written large upon these pages of revelation... Let no man suppose that progress can be divorced from religion, or that there is any other platform for the ministers of reform than the platform written in the utterances of our Lord and Savior. America was born a Christian nation. America was born to exemplify that devotion to the elements of righteousness which are derived from the revelations of Holy Scripture. [37]

Today we hear a lot of talk about America being a pluralistic society. If we mean by this that many different beliefs make up the American population, we are indeed a pluralistic group. America is a place where people of all religions and persuasions (including atheism), may freely believe what they so choose. But if we mean by pluralism that a single belief system, in particular, a Bible-based system, should not be the basis of our laws and civil institutions, we are taking a totally opposite direction in our thinking than the founding fathers had in mind. This way of thinking is relatively new, and we must not assume that it is a historic American ideal. It simply is not. E.R. Norman, an English historian, said, "pluralism is a word society employs during the transition from one orthodoxy to another." [38]

This has certainly been the case in America over the past fifty years. Some may think that morality can be brought back into our nation without bringing back a respect for the Bible and the principles it contains. But George Washington said, "reason and experience both forbid us to expect that national morality can prevail in exclusion of religious principle." [39] Where do you think the "religious principle" he had in mind was found? In none other than the Book the founding fathers quoted more often than any other – the Bible. The Book President Abraham Lincoln affirmed, by declaring: "In regard to this Great Book, I have but to say, it is the best gift God has given man. All the good the Savior gave to the world was communicated through this book. But for it we could not know right from wrong." [40]

Now, why would John Adams say our constitution is wholly inadequate for the governing of any other than a moral and religious people? It is because these kind of people know how to govern themselves under God, and people who govern themselves under God do not need kings, dictators, or potentates to regulate their actions. People who are morally responsible internally do not need the external strong arm of government to tell them what they can or cannot do. People with self-government, or self-control, understand what is required of them to live at peace with others. Furthermore, self-control is not just a matter of restraining evil impulses, but of initiating good without being manipulated to do so. The essence of genuine moral self-government is to be motivated by internalized principles of godliness.

Strong, external governmental control was precisely what the founding fathers were trying to get away from, and what they did not want repeated on the west side of the Atlantic. But with a "moral and religious" population, a government "by the people" might just work. Individuals with moral self-government under God would bring peace, order, and, as Washington put it, "political prosperity" to a new kind of governmental system. This was a revolutionary, biblically-based idea. Free speech could be entrusted to such a populace, as could the freedom of the press and even the right to bear arms.

Daniel Webster summed it up this way: "Our ancestors established their system of government on morality and religious sentiment. Moral habits, they believed, cannot safely be trusted on any other foundation than religious principle, nor any government be secure which is not supported by moral habits. Living under the heavenly light of revelation, they hoped to find all the social dispositions, all the duties which men owe to each other and to society, enforced and performed. Whatever makes men good Christians, makes them good citizens." [41]

Today we still have the form of a free nation, but we are rapidly losing the character necessary to sustain it. Our civil freedoms can only survive as long as the American people are able to govern themselves in a morally responsible way. While no freedom-granting government can keep people morally responsible, only morally responsible people can keep government freedom-granting. The more Americans there are who do not practice moral self-government, the greater risk we all have of losing what freedoms we yet enjoy. The choice is simple: Either the American people will regain their ability to morally govern themselves from the internal side of things, or the strong arm of government will come in and control us from the external side of things. Benjamin Franklin said, "Only a virtuous people are capable of freedom. As nations become corrupt and vicious, they have more need of masters." [42] Robert Winthrop put it this way, in 1852: "Men, in a word, must necessarily be controlled either by a power within them, or by a power without them; either by the Word of God, or by the strong arm of man, either by the Bible, or by the bayonet." [43]

In the America of 1787, when the Constitution was first drafted, it was not unreasonable to think Americans would be the kind of moral and religious people necessary for this freedom-granting kind of government to work. Early Americans, especially the educated, were Bible-conscious, and understood what moral self-government under God was all about. After all, they had sacrificed much to gain the opportunity to freely practice it.

Here is what Calvin Coolidge had to say about it:

America became the common meeting-place of all those streams of people, great and small, who were undertaking to deliver themselves from all kinds of despotism and servitude, and to establish institutions of self-government and freedom... It was the principle of personal judgment in matters of religion for which the English and Dutch were contending, and which set the common people to reading the Bible. There came to them a new vision of the importance of the individual which brought him into direct contact with the Creator. It was this conception applied to affairs of government that made the people sovereign... The logical result of this was the free man, educated in a free school, exercising a free conscience, maintaining a free government. The basis of it all, historically and logically, is religious belief.

These are the fundamental principles on which American institutions rest... It was the American colonies that defended and reestablished these everlasting truths. They set them out in resolutions and declarations, supported them on the battlefield, wrote them into their laws, and adopted them in their Constitution.[44]

Of course not all Americans were Christians, by any means. And those who were Christians were not faultless. But the overriding thrust of the colonies, and the new nation that followed, was openly Bible-based and Christian oriented. The following official statement issued by the House Judiciary Committee of Congress on March 27, 1854, bears this out: "At the time of the adoption of the Constitution and the amendments, the universal sentiment was that Christianity should be encouraged, but not any one sect... In this age there is no substitute for Christianity... That was the religion of the founders of the republic, and they expected it to remain the religion of their descendants."[45] And two months later, the following was declared by the Committee: "The great, vital, and conservative element in our system is the belief of our people in the pure doctrines and divine truths of the Gospel of Jesus Christ."[46]

The very basis of law in early America was openly founded upon the Bible, as seen in the *Commentaries* of William Blackstone, an English jurist who greatly influenced the colonists. He wrote from the assumption that God is the source of all authority, and that His Word rests above all other words, even those of kings. His *Commentaries* clearly leaned upon Scripture for support. This is evident in even a casual glance at his work, which for many years was the standard text for lawyers trained in early America.

The historical evidence for Christianity as the compelling force behind American laws and civil institutions is so weighty that when the United States Supreme Court had occasion to look into this matter, in the case of Church of the Holy Trinity v. United States (1892), the court issued the following statement, quoting no less than eighty-seven precedents:

Our laws and our institutions must necessarily be based upon and embody the teachings of The Redeemer of mankind. It is impossible that it should be otherwise; and in this sense and to this extent our civilization and our institutions are emphatically Christian... This is a religious people. This is historically true. From the discovery of this continent to the present hour, there is a single voice making this affirmation... we find everywhere a clear recognition of the same truth... These, and many other matters which might be noticed, add a volume of unofficial declarations to the mass of organic utterances that this is a Christian nation.[47]

Many people are uncomfortable with the term "Christian nation," and for good reason. The phrase itself is a misnomer in the sense that a country can never be "Christian." Only individual people within nations can be Christian. But in using this descriptive language in connection with America, the court was not saying everybody born in this country was a Christian, nor was the Court saying this nation existed just for Christians, nor were they saying that no other religions should be freely practiced in America. But what the 1892 Court did clearly say was, our laws and institutions "must necessarily be based upon and embody the teachings of The Redeemer of mankind... and in this sense and to this extent our civilization and our institutions are emphatically Christian."

How far we have drifted! To say that our culture is emphatically Christian today would be blasphemy. Our revised laws are no longer based upon the teachings of Jesus, as it was once said by the Supreme Court they should be. But the point of this chapter is simply this: it was once thought they should be! The question that naturally comes to mind is, why do we hear so much talk today about the "separation of church and state?"

This is a very important question, and deserves special consideration.

## SEPARATION OF CHURCH AND STATE

Ask the man on the street where the phrase "separation of church and state" comes from and you will likely be told it comes from the Constitution of the United States. After all, we're repeatedly reminded these days that it's unconstitutional to mix Christianity with civil government. The more astute man on the street may tell you the phrase comes from the First Amendment to the Constitution.

But in reality, this well-known phrase, which often appears in our newspapers and seems to be engraved upon the minds of all Americans, does not appear in the Constitution at all, neither in the document drafted in Philadelphia in 1787, nor in the First Amendment later adopted by Congress in 1789. What the First Amendment actually says, with regard to the matter of religion is: "Congress shall make no law respecting an establishment of religion, or prohibiting the free exercise thereof."

But in spite of the fact that the words "separation of church and state" do not appear in the Constitution, there is an important truth contained in the concept of separation of church and state which the founding fathers knew was important. They wisely recognized that no man can be forced to conform to a particular religious belief, and Congress should be forbidden from even trying to do such a thing. They had seen enough religious compulsion in Europe, and its bad effects. America was to be a place where a man was free to decide for himself which church he would be a part of. More than that, America was a place where a man could choose to be a part of no church, if he so pleased.

The First Amendment was specifically adopted to insure freedom from coercion by the church through civil means. It was designed to keep any single denomination of Christianity from controlling all others through state power. And at the same time, Congress was forever forbidden from interfering with the right of the American people to freely exercise their religious convictions as individuals. Yet, the First Amendment was certainly not intended to divorce Christian principles from civil government.

Yes, there is a rightful separation of church and state in the sense of function and jurisdiction. The church should not administer justice to criminals. This is the civil government's duty. The civil government should not baptize believers. This is the duty of the church. The church should not be ruling over the state any more than the state should be interfering with what goes on in the church. While the government of God extends over everything in heaven and earth, both church and state included, the government of church has definite limits beyond which it must not overstep. The Bible does not teach an ecclesiocracy, or "rule of the church," over other institutions such as the family or the state. God does intend, however, for churches as well as civil governments to both function under His authority. Both have equal accountability under God.

One cannot legitimately separate God from civil government any more than one can separate God from church government. He is equally Lord of both. At the same time, one can and should separate church government from civil government. Here is the crux of some confusion, even among Christians. There is a big difference between separation of church and state, and separation of God and government. But, you may ask, if the founding fathers did not advocate a separation of Christian principles from civil government, where did the phrase "separation of church and state" come from, and why is it interpreted today as meaning a separation of Christian principles from civil affairs?

The phrase "separation of church and state" came from a short letter written by Thomas Jefferson, in response to a group of Baptists in Danbury, Connecticut, who heard a false report that the national government was going to make the Congregationalist denomination the official denomination of America. Jefferson assured the Baptists they had nothing to fear, by telling them there was a "wall of separation between church and state." This is true, in terms of respective spheres of function and jurisdiction. But today, the phrase "separation of church and state" has become, in essence, a much bantered call for the elimination of any semblance of Christianity from civil affairs. Is this what Jefferson had in mind? If it were, do you think this is a message the President would have sent to the Danbury Baptists? Of course not. Certainly he would not have wanted to antagonize a group of Baptists by telling them basic Christian principles have no place in civil government. Not in 1802.

Well, then, how have Jefferson's words "separation of church and state" come to mean what they do to most Americans today? Historian David Barton, writing in *The Myth of Separation*, points out that it is largely the result of an extraordinary ruling by the U.S. Supreme Court in 1947, in *Everson v. Board of Education*.[48] Here the Court cited the eight words of Jefferson's letter, about "a wall of separation between church and state," and announced: "The First Amendment has erected 'a wall of separation between church and state.' That wall must be kept high and impregnable."[49] The Court used these words to support a ruling to forbid religious practices from public affairs. This action was taken without precedent!

After the 1947 case, the Court often referred to the phrase "separation of church and state," and in 1962 interpreted the word "church," in the phrase "separation of church and state" to mean "a religious activity in public." With this interpretation, the Court struck down prayer in public schools. This present day interpretation of the doctrine of separation of church and state is a relatively new interpretation, which had zero historical precedent prior to 1962. But since that time, we have seen repeated cases in which the Supreme Court has used this new interpretation to justify decisions which the very framers of the First Amendment would have viewed with dumbfounded amazement.

Separation of church and state? Of course, in terms of function and juris-diction. But separation of God and government? Try convincing God of that. It is no accident that American churches have been given a unique opportunity to flourish apart from civil encroachment. It is also no accident that American churches are exempt from paying taxes. It is in the best interests of the entire nation that churches are given every possible advantage to prosper. This makes abundant sense when you realize, as John Adams did, that the whole future of the American system rests upon the continuing existence of a body of people who practice moral self-government under God. How could such a people be insured for the future unless the church was free to do its work in encouraging and equipping people to live out their Christianity in American homes, schools, and communities?

In the early days of our country, this was one of the primary purposes behind schools, too. In fact, schools were usually an extension of the church. In the 1830s, when de Tocqueville came from France to examine America, he noted "almost all education is entrusted to the clergy." [50] Most schools were established by Christians for Christian purposes. With the exception of the University of Pennsylvania, every collegiate institution founded in the colonies prior to the Revolutionary War was established by some branch of the Christian church. These include Harvard, Yale, Princeton, Dartmouth, and Rutgers University. And after the Revolutionary War, the planting of schools by Christians continued.

One of the most significant American educators, Noah Webster (born in 1758) felt strongly that education was to play a critical role in shaping the morally self-governing character of the American populace. He once said, "the education of youth should be watched with the most scrupulous attention. Education, in a great measure, forms the moral characters of men, and morals are the basis of government." He went on to say, "it is much easier to introduce and establish an effectual system for preserving morals, than to correct, by penal statutes, the ill effects of a bad system." [51] How true!

Once again, you can be assured the morals Webster was referring to were specifically Bible based, and you can be certain Webster believed Christianity was to mix with civil government. In a letter written on October 25, 1836, to David McClure, he wrote the following remarkable words:

No truth is more evident to my mind than that the Christian religion must be the basis of any government intended to secure the rights and privileges of a free people... When I speak of the Christian religion as the basis of government... I mean primitive Christianity in its simplicity as taught by Christ and His apostles, consisting in a belief in the being, perfections, and moral government of God; in the revelation of His will to men, as their supreme rule of action; in man's... accountability to God for his conduct in this life; and in the indispensable obligation of all men to yield entire obedience to God's commands in the moral law and in the Gospel... The foundation of all free government and all social order must be laid in families and in the discipline of youth. Young persons must not only be furnished with knowledge, but they must be accustomed to subordination and subjected to the authority and influence of good principles. It will avail little that youths are made to understand truth and correct principles, unless they are accustomed to submit to be governed by them... And any system of education... which limits instruction to the arts and sciences, and rejects the aids of religion in forming the character of citizens, is essentially defective.

How precisely Mr. Webster has put his finger on the heart of our problem today! He goes on in his letter to affirm the Bible as "that book which the benevolent Creator has furnished for the express purpose of guiding human reason in the path of safety, and the only book which can remedy, or essentially mitigate, the evils of a licentious world." [52]

Spoken with the precision of a man who understood the need for clear communication, Webster's words are those we would do well to take to heart today!

**CHAPTER SIX SUMMARY: KEY PEOPLE, PLACES AND CONCEPTS**
The privatization of Christianity
The Kingdom of God
The distinctive roles of church and state
Ecclesiocracy
Thomas Jefferson (1743-1826)

*For Further Thought and Discussion*

1. Discuss the practical results of limiting the "sacred" realm of life to church-related activities or activities of an eternal nature.

2. Clarify in your own words the meaning of "separation of church and state."

3. Explain why Noah Webster and other early American leaders believed Christianity was essential to the success of the American experiment in civil government.

4. What influence has the notion of "privatized religion" had upon education in America?

# Chapter Seven

# A Hebraic Education

I n September of 1989, George Bush Sr. did something no other U.S. President had done. He called the nation's governors together to promote educational reform, calling national attention to the needy condition of our public schools. Never in the history of America has there been so much talk about the need for an overhaul of education as there has been since the mid-1980s. The cry has not been just from private school critics, but from public educators themselves, and the nation's business community, who painfully recognize we have a serious problem on our hands.

But the root problem of our schools is not a problem we can fix through legislative mandates. The problem behind our failing schools is the same problem behind our failing homes. It is a problem of failing ethics, failing morality, and failing spiritual eyesight. Significant and lasting educational reform requires ethical, moral, and spiritual reform, which will produce a reform of our assumptions, and thus a reform in our way of educating.

In the meantime, educators are searching for models of education that produce good fruit. In view of the present need, the question which naturally comes is, "What does the Hebrew model have to offer educators today?"

While the Bible has little to say directly about schools, it has some very important things to say about learning, knowledge, pupils, and teachers. Hebraic tradition has much to say about these things as well. The comments expressed in this chapter are made in an attempt to describe the essence of the Hebrew model, not necessarily the form through which it might express itself. In other words, certain principles are suggested here, while the particular expression of these principles may take a variety of shapes, sizes, and environments, both public and private. It is, after all, the essence of the Hebrew model which sets this philosophy of life and education apart from others, and breathes into it a spirit of a different kind than we may have grown accustomed to today. It certainly is a different kind than one would have encountered in ancient Greece.

When Plutarch, the Greek historian, describes Sparta as a place where "no one was allowed to live after his own fancy; but the city was a sort of camp, in which every man... served the interests of his country," you get a feel for what the aim of education in Sparta was all about. Theologian William Barclay wrote that education in Sparta was for "the obliteration of the individual in the service of the state."

In Athens, of course, things were much different. Here, in the free thinking land of philosophers and artists, the individual was anything but obliterated, and education served another purpose. Whereas Spartan education was completely regulated by the state for the purpose of training citizens for the service of their country, Athenian education was almost entirely individualistic. Schools were organized by private enterprise, with no regulation as to the subject matter taught, although most schools concentrated on literature, music, and gymnastics. Barclay said education in Athens was for "the training of the individual in the service of culture."

For the ancient Hebrew, education had a much different goal. Among the Jews, Barclay wrote, education was for "the training of the individual in the service of God." [53]

But whether in Sparta, Athens, or Jerusalem, one thing remains the same: the convictions, values, and goals which are most important to a particular group of people become the motivating force behind educating the next generation. At least that is the way it must be if education is to be true to the group it serves. An authentic approach to education springs from a philosophy of life. This is certainly the case with the Hebrew model.

With this in mind, it is no surprise that a biblical model of educating the next generation begins with family, in the context of a home where two people, a father and a mother, who are committed to love one another until death does them part, view the child as a temporary addition to the home to be nurtured and trained in self-government under God. This is done so the son or daughter may be sent out from that home one day with confidence and joy. The

Hebrew model of education, then, starts with parents who see themselves as responsible for shaping that soft clay into a morally self-governing person, who is teachable and prepared to learn.

Properly functioning homes are the foundation of an effective educational system. When homes fall apart, so do schools. We cannot hope to see a repair of our schools apart from a repair of our homes. Trying to do so is like laying new kitchen tile over rotten floor boards.

Have you ever painted a house? Or put in a new kitchen floor? If you have, you understand the meaning of the word "preparation." Scraping the old paint off and masking the windows and doors, or removing the old floor cover and fixing any damaged wood underneath, is usually the most difficult part of the whole job. And it is so necessary for good results.

When it comes to educating children, the prep work cannot be minimized or underestimated. Preparing children for learning includes training them in such basic skills as listening when an adult is speaking, honoring the one giving instruction, prompt obedience, respect for others, and self-control. These are not qualities children are born with. Yet they are foundational learning skills which can and should be operative in normal children, properly trained at home, prior to formal education.

Now many readers may be saying, "That sounds great, but it just isn't reality in today's American culture." How true! That's just the point. Remember, we're not looking to today's American culture for models. Today's culture is the problem, not the solution. We're talking here about how to change things. Furthermore, as more and more young parents are saying "no" to the post-World War II models of child-centered parenting which has produced the most destructive, me-centered generation in American history, an increasing number of parents are taking a different approach, one that sees what has just been described above as normal. Which brings us to a second major component of the Hebrew model, namely, a community of families with a commonly-held worldview, mutually-applied standards of parenting, and agreed-upon purposes for learning.

Even more rare today than an individual family with a biblical approach to parenting and learning is a community of such families. But when you have this, you have the potential for a dynamic kind of education. A kind of education in which "school" is not the center of education, per se, but rather the community of families, or "village," which collectively form a body of responsible participants.

In past chapters we have addressed the issues of worldviews and parenting practices. These are not things to pass over lightly, but we do not have space to repeat them here. We need only to realize that educating the next generation takes place within a much broader context than the student-teacher relationship alone. The "village" is much broader, and the Hebrews felt it took an entire one to raise a child.

Although the idea of the village has been popularized in the media in recent years, the modern view of the village usually refers to a network of social workers or state and federal government programs as the caretakers of children. The Hebrew concept of village referred to a network of caring family and friends, who share the same values.

With this as a backdrop, we will now look at the third element we've mentioned, namely, united purposes for learning. The principal aim of learning, according to the Proverbs, is to gain wisdom and understanding: "Wisdom is the principal thing; therefore get wisdom. And in all your getting, get understanding." (Proverbs 4:7) Wisdom is not to be confused with intellectual skill or ability. It is entirely possible for a person to have a high IQ score and yet be very unwise. The opposite is also true. The "smart" are not necessarily the wise. And in striving to be smart, many have succeeded in becoming educated fools. Many no longer know how to live as they ought. In this respect we have detached school from life, and learning from living. The Hebrew model will not permit this. The very meaning of the word wisdom requires something much different.

Abraham Heschel, respected Jewish author, once wrote, "To us, wisdom is the ability to look at all things from the point of view of God." [54] This is a much different starting point than for Socrates, Plato, and Aristotle. For the Greek, education began and ended with man and his mannish concerns. Whether it was the individual man, as in Athens, or the collective man, as in Sparta, man was the measure of all things, including education. "Know thyself" was Socrates' cry, while "know God" was the cry of the Hebrew.

This knowing of God and seeing all things from His point of view required getting to know what He said, and what He thought. The process began very early in the life of the Hebrew child. Formal instruction ordinarily began in the home, when the child was about three years old. At five years of age, study of the Hebrew Bible began. Little parchment rolls, made especially for use by children, contained the following portions of Scripture: the Shema (Deuteronomy 6:4-9; 11:13-21; Numbers 15:37-41); the Hallel (Psalm 113-118); the account of creation, the Fall, and the genealogy from Adam to Noah (Genesis 1-5); and the essence of the Levitical Law (Leviticus 1-8).

Within these passages lie all the basic elements of a biblical worldview: the origin of life through the intelligent act of a personal-unlimited Creator; the identity of man as an image-bearer of God, yet fallen through sin; his call to responsible stewardship over the earth; the supreme authority of God, and the absolute, non-negotiableness of moral law as something to recognize and accept, rather than determine for oneself; the centrality of a love relationship with God; the role of parents as teachers in the lives of their children; the promise of blessing upon those who love and serve Him; the foolishness of serving idols; and more.

You can be sure these Scriptures were not just an exercise in memorization. Parents were expected to instruct their children as they sat in their homes, walked along the way, went to bed, and rose up in the morning (Deut. 6:7). It was the duty of fathers to take an active role in instructing their children, as was first expected of Abraham, a man God recognized would command his children after him, in order that Israel might become a mighty nation (Genesis 18:19).

This is not to say that all instruction had to come from the father, but, as Abraham Heschel points out, any teacher outside of the home was to be viewed as a representative of the father himself.[55] With this in mind, it is understandable that the first question a Jew would have asked about a teacher would not have been, "What kind of a scholar is he?" but, "What kind of a person is he?" After all, a pupil, to be fully trained by a teacher, was not merely seen as having a head full of similar facts, but actually being like his teacher (Luke 6:40). Because of this, the Hebrew model not only places a priority upon a student's genuine respect for a teacher as someone to be honored and listened to at all times, but also places a priority upon the genuine respectability of teachers as the kind of people parents would not hesitate to have their children imitate, being those who exemplify the moral character they want to see in their own sons and daughters.

The Hebrew model of education rests upon a moral base, not an academic one. That is to say, virtue (moral excellence) is the foundation upon which all skill and academic ability is to be built. For knowledge apart from virtue is vanity. Worse than that, adding knowledge to those void of virtue is a violation of good sense. As someone aptly put it, "The world already has enough educated fools."

This is not to say that facts are unimportant, nor that the transfer of information is of no value, nor that intellectual pursuit is wrong. Of course not. Yet, for many American students, education is little more than a matter of information being transferred, and learning is reduced to the accumulation of facts, or the development of certain mental and physical skills. Marvin Wilson, in *The Jewish Concept of Learning: A Christian Appreciation,* notes:

In the Greek world, teaching primarily involved the transference of knowledge in the intellectual and technical areas, e.g. music, art, riding, reading or fencing. Thus, a teacher taught his pupil certain rules or procedures which hopefully would help to develop any aptitude that pupil might possess. If his reasoning powers needed development, then intellectual exercises were provided; if his body needed training, then sports and physical exercise were stressed; if greater manual dexterity was needed, then art or sculpturing might be taught. In short, in secular Greek literature, the *didaskalos,* or "teacher," aimed mainly at developing the talents and potentialities of his pupil. Unlike the idea of teaching in the Jewish world, his teaching did not usually concern itself with the development of his student's whole personality, and his education in the deepest sense.[56]

Modern educators have somehow imparted the Greek notion that students are educated through the development of mental capacity and rational or technical skills. But to see such things as the primary purpose of education while neglecting personal virtue is, as Webster put it, "essentially defective."

It is not a matter of stressing one or the other, but simply stressing both, with the understanding that knowledge and virtue must go hand in glove. Knowledge being the glove, and virtue being the hand that fills it, directs it, and employs it for proper purposes.

Not surprisingly, in an atmosphere where virtue is laid as a foundation to knowledge, it's remarkable how much knowledge will actually be found! In an environment where students practice principles of self-government (i.e., self-control), not only can a teacher accomplish a great deal of teaching, but students can accomplish a great deal of learning. It is an element currently missing from a great many American classrooms, but in the early years of our nation it was considered quite normal.

A brief look at early American education would be helpful at this point. Not only was virtue an expected part of education, but early Americans had another purpose for learning which must be included in a biblical model, namely, the equipping of people for responsible stewardship under God in all of life, whether public or private, civil or domestic. We can learn much from the example of early American education.

### DID THE PURITANS KNOW SOMETHING WE DON'T?

When you hear the word puritanical, what comes to your mind? Whatever comes to mind, it's probably not positive. This illustrates the unfortunate fact that in the minds of most Americans, the Puritans are viewed as people not to be like. They are generally thought of as prudish, unfashionable, workaholics, who were against sex, opposed to fun and laughter, and oppressively legalistic.

But the fact of the matter is, the Puritans have been given a historic smear. As Leland Ryken, professor of English at Wheaton College, put it: "No group of people has been more unjustly maligned in the twentieth century than the Puritans. As a result, we approach the Puritans with an enormous baggage of culturally ingrained prejudice." [57] Ryken lays out in very specific terms where our image of the Puritans is accurate, and where it is not, with a remarkable amount of original source documentation. The truth is, more often than not, we are off base in our popular images of these people.

While it would not be good to over-elevate the Puritans, all Americans owe a debt of gratitude to them. We would do well to take a closer look at what they really believed and how they really behaved. This is particularly true when searching for historic examples of a Hebraic approach to education, for there is not a better example of a people forging a biblical philosophy of life into education than the Puritans.

When John Milton, the famous Puritan leader of seventeenth century England, came to putting his thoughts on education in writing, he said: "The end then of learning is to repair the ruins of our first parents by regaining to know God aright, and out of that knowledge to love Him, to imitate Him, to be like Him, as we may the nearest by possessing our souls of true virtue...." [58] Milton's words capture the bottom line of the Hebrew model. He does not talk about education as a means of merely developing the brains, the talents, and potential of the individual, but sees it in terms of the kind of person the learner is becoming.

Yet, Milton does not advocate some sort of introspective, mystical, religious detachment from life. His reasons for becoming "like God" are very practical and down to earth: "I call therefore a complete and generous education that which fits a man to perform justly, skillfully, and magnanimously, all the offices, both private and public, of peace and war." [59]

It doesn't get any more all-inclusive than this. Such was the Puritan vision of life. They were compelled by the desire to see the application of pure, practical Christianity throughout all of life, public or private, whether in the home, the church, at work, or in civil affairs. They stood against the religious trappings of the Church of England at great cost, and many came to the New World to see if indeed the vision could become reality.

As a result, Puritan education not only sought to prepare godly pastors and parents, but godly civil servants and citizens of all sorts, who had the moral integrity to govern justly and harmoniously under God. In this way a person was seen to be a truly beneficial citizen and productive member of society.

For the Puritan, social and cultural involvement was expected, and the natural outgrowth of a worldview which saw all of life as sacred, and everything under the dominion of God. Not to be involved responsibly in the culture would have been irresponsible. And as far as the colonial American Puritan experiment was concerned, they knew the eyes of the world were upon them. Because of this, John Winthrop said, "We must consider that we shall be as a city upon a hill." It was in the New World they had a chance to put their worldview into practice, and they were not about to miss the opportunity.

It is then no surprise that the Puritans saw value in all spheres of knowledge, and did not limit themselves to only so-called "religious" concerns. Such a sacred-secular split was happily absent from their mentality, and as a result they pursued all types of legitimate study, keeping it all subject to the final authority of Scripture. It was because of their affirmation of all of creation that the Puritans were able to have a balanced appreciation for both the physical as well as the spiritual aspects of life. As a result, they valued not only book learning, but bench making as well. In no way did they demean manual labor, but were able to say, as one of them did, that a Christian can regard "his shop as well as his chapel as holy ground." [60]

We should note here that craftsmen and artisans who made furniture and garments for the Tabernacle of Moses were said to have been "endowed with the spirit of wisdom" (Exodus 28:3). This leads us to the understanding that wisdom is more than thought or spoken words, and can find its expression through skillful craftsmanship as well. What's more, all work is a sacred task when done "as unto the Lord" (Colossians 3:23), be it preaching or painting.

The Puritans were intensely motivated by a vision to see God rightfully honored in all of life. While at times their zeal got the best of them, and produced an unfortunate extremism in certain respects, they were on the right track in most regards. When it comes to education, their purpose was one which present day Americans would do well to remember. If God's rightful jurisdiction is over all facets of law, politics, business, science, the arts, labor, and family, then the role of education is abundantly obvious. Today, more than ever, we are in need not only of godly pastors and Bible teachers, but also godly lawyers, politicians, diplomats, judges, doctors, economists, educators, artists, carpenters, mechanics, and used car salesmen who see their jobs as a way to honorably represent God's ways in daily living.

A biblically-based model of education must concern itself with the application of wisdom to every branch of learning. As Daniel, the Hebrew who served four gentile kings in Babylon, showed "intelligence in every branch of wisdom, endowed with understanding, and discerning knowledge" (Daniel 1:4), so, too, Christians today must be concerned with equipping the next generation for service in the world in which they live.

In Daniel's case, three years of intensive education in the literature and language of the Chaldeans were required in preparation for King Nebuchadnezzar's personal service. At the end of this time, Daniel and his friends were found to be ten times better than all the king's magicians and conjurers in every matter of wisdom and understanding in which he consulted them (Daniel 1:20). Daniel's wise counsel was sought out by kings who did not know God, because even unbelievers appreciate genuine wisdom when they see it. It's the same today.

If Christians are going to occupy positions of influence in our culture, they must not only understand the Word of God, but "the language and literature of the Chaldeans" as well. For example, if we are going to have an effect upon civil government once again, we must do so with trained and skillful men and women who understand the language and literature of the political process, the economic system, U.S. history, world affairs, and public relations. We need more than those who would say "Vote for me because I am a Christian." Being a Christian is not enough. And if we are going to see a return of our legal base to godly standards (and we should), we must have judges and lawmakers who not only understand the language and literature of our legal system, but are able to speak with ten times the wisdom of all the legal magicians and conjurers of our current courts.

If there ever was a time for Christians to move out of their trenches, it is now. The purpose of education must be directed toward equipping whole people to bring the righteousness, peace, and joy of God's kingdom not only to our personal lives, but also out into whatever sphere of reality our hands and minds are cultivating, be it in the aerospace industry or a potato chip factory, the world of the arts, or the U.S. Supreme Court. Christians, of all people, should be vibrant cultivators of creation, because we know and love the Landowner personally. This is what gave the Puritans their vigor throughout the totality of life, and gave education a vital purpose, meaning, and significance.

The concern of early American Christians for education as a means to honor God throughout the whole spectrum of life was what drove them to establish schools. Yale, for example, was established in 1701 to be an institution where "youth may be instructed in the Arts and Sciences who through the blessing of Almighty God may be fitted for Public employment both in Church and Civil State."[61]

Somewhere along the way, the guiding purpose of early American educators began to shift, until today we find it hard to believe that the schools these people sacrificed to start were once the offspring of Bible-based Christianity. As the privatization of Christianity and the imbalanced focus upon the after-life began to infiltrate the thinking of Christians, the effects upon American education were debilitating and far reaching. As the people of God steered away from involvement in cultural and civil affairs, a spirit of a much different type came in to fill the void.

## HOW DID WE GET SO FAR OFF TRACK?

On September 12, 1905, five men gathered at Peck's Restaurant, 140 Fulton Street, in lower Manhattan, for the purpose of discussing how to bring about a different social order for America. Among the five present that day were Upton Sinclair, Jack London, and Clarence Darrow. Meeting in a loft above the restaurant, they gave birth to an organization called the Intercollegiate Socialist Society. Their plans to effect social change included the establishment of chapters of the organization on college campuses throughout the nation.

By 1912, 44 colleges and universities had such chapters, and by 1917, 61 schools of higher learning had chapters, as well as a dozen graduate schools. In 1921, the name of the organization was changed to the League for Industrial Democracy, with its specific purpose being "education for a new social order." By the mid-1930s, 125 units of the organization were in place. At this time, John Dewey was the League's vice president, and in 1941 he became its president.[62]

The information given in this chapter is not meant to imply that the exchange of America's predominantly Christian worldview for a much different way of thinking sprang solely from a meeting of five men in a loft above Peck's restaurant. Such an undertaking required much more than this, and it began much earlier. But the effects such men had upon our educational system, beginning at the university level and proceeding down from there, greatly sped the process along.

In colonial America there was no distinction between public and private schools on the basis of "secular" versus "religious" grounds. Basically, all schools, whether public or private, were based on the idea that religion and education were inseparable.

As time went on, the prominence of Puritanism began to fade as the rising tide of the Enlightenment reached the shores of the New World, eventually leading to a rejection of revelation-based faith and an acceptance of reason-based faith. Reason-based faith entered Christianity in the form of deism. Deism claimed that while God did create the world, at the same time He equipped man with a mind so that he could determine what was right and wrong by means of his own reason. The Bible was only true to the extent that it was in harmony with reason. Instead of submitting reason to revelation, deism reversed the order, and submitted revelation to reason. Deists denied that the Scriptures were the infallible Word of God, and did not accept the doctrine of the Fall, nor of redemption through Christ.

Deism incorporated the idea that the world was governed by "natural law." In the deistic view, God was only needed to get things going in the beginning. Once this was accomplished, He stepped aside and let the world go ahead on its own, with things proceeding quite "naturally," with man finding morality and goodness by means of his own sense of right and wrong. Following the assumption that reason was a fully adequate guide to truth, reason eventually reasoned out both God and the Bible altogether. For the deist, final authority was not in an objective source of revelation, i.e., the Bible, but in the hands of man and "Nature."

The replacement of the God of the Bible with "Nature" [capital N] in the eighteenth and nineteenth centuries was a critical factor in the change of direction taken by Western thought, just as it was for the Greeks some two thousand years earlier. The deism of the eighteenth century led to a variety of other "isms," including Darwinism, humanism, social pragmatism, and existentialism.

It only required a small step to go from deism to Darwinism. After all, if God only got things going in the beginning, and man does not need Him or His revelation to live by, then God may as well be dead anyway. But there had to be some explanation for life on planet earth as we know it, didn't there? It couldn't have just happened on its own, could it?

Charles Darwin's popularization of the theory of evolution provided the necessary "scientific" answer that allowed men to drop the idea of God in a reasonable, rational, and publicly acceptable manner. Through *On the Origin of Species* (1859), and *The Descent of Man* (1891), Charles Darwin brought evolutionary theory into the mainstream of popular thought.

Evolution was accepted by scientists, artists, philosophers, as well as theologians. It was seen as not only a physical phenomena, but a social, religious, and economical one as well. Few, if any, ideas have had a greater impact upon the modern world as has the theory of evolution. The acceptance of this idea opened the door for many changes in social behavior and cultural standards. The incorporation of these changes into education took place largely through the work of John Dewey, the gentleman mentioned previously who became the president of the League for Industrial Democracy.

John Dewey (1859-1952) is sometimes called the Father of American Progressive Education. He was not only perhaps the most influential educator in modern American history, but he has also been recognized as a world-class philosopher. As the head of Teacher's College, Columbia University (1904-1930), Dewey was able to make a lasting impact upon a whole generation of American teachers and heads of other colleges of education.

Dewey's ideas were greatly influenced by the work of William James (1842-1910), who carried the Darwinian revolution into the field of psychology. James began from the assumption that truth was relative, always in a state of change and never in a fixed or absolute state. Truth, according to James, "happens to an idea," ever evolving and ever in process. It is not "final" in an ultimate sense. Truth is something which changes and continues to adapt to fit its environment. So it happens that truths which once may have been fitting to a particular social environment may not be fitting today. Only the fittest truths survive, and if it doesn't fit, it is no longer truth. Truth is what works. This way of thinking, called pragmatism, is America's distinctive (and destructive) contribution to the stream of Western philosophic thought.

Dewey sought to forge the philosophy of social pragmatism into the backbone of American public education. He was concerned with the progressive evolution of ideas affecting society as a whole, and sought to help the process along through "progressive" education. The public school, of course, was the natural place for idea changes to take place. What better place could be found than the fertile soil of youth? Change requires a certain suppleness of mind, and young minds lend themselves better to this process. According to the social pragmatist, then, the school is to be a facilitator of change.

According to pragmatism, society itself becomes the determining factor of what is truly fitting for the age in which it lives. Right and wrong, true and false are relative to the current needs and aspirations of the group. What is good is what works. As American culture changes, America's values change. As America's values change, American culture changes, and so the evolutionary process of progressive truth goes on and on.

Progressive education resists the idea of unchanging dogmas such as those taught by the Bible. The very word "dogma" has a negative connotation. The idea of absolute, unchanging values is shunned, and people who hold to them are often called "intolerant" or "narrow-minded." Education for the progressive educator, then, is that process by which a person learns to be "open-minded," or "reasonable." Reason, of course, is the true guiding light in determining right and wrong. People who base their ideas on revelation are considered to be unenlightened mental cripples, with the Bible as their crutch.

In *My Pedagogic Creed*, Dewey referred to the teacher as "the prophet of the true God and the usherer of the true kingdom of God." [63] He dispensed with the idea of a Creator and had no room for absolute morals or the supernatural. "Nature" was the ultimate reality. Dewey did not try to conceal the fact that his way of thinking was indeed a faith, a nontheistic faith, but a faith nonetheless. In his appropriately titled book, *A Common Faith*, Dewey described "the ideal ends to which we attach our faith" as having "all the elements for a religious faith that shall not be confined to sect, class, or race." [64]

Dewey's faith was in a religion called Humanism.[65] He served as the president of the American Humanist Association, which in 1933 published the *Humanist Manifesto I,* a document which outlined the basic tenets of the faith in a clear and concise manner. Forty years later, the American Humanist Association published the *Humanist Manifesto II* (1973). *Humanist Manifesto III* was published in 1999. The following selections from these manifestos speak for themselves:

Religious humanists regard the universe as self-existing and not created. (Affirmation 1, H.M.I) Humanism believes that man is a part of nature and that he has emerged as the result of a continuous process. (Affirmation 2, H.M.I)

We believe... that traditional... religions that place revelation, God, ritual or creed above human needs and experience do a disservice... We find insufficient evidence for belief in the existence of a supernatural; As non-theists, we begin with humans, not God, nature, not deity. We can discover no divine purpose or providence for the human species... humans are responsible for what we are or will become. No deity will save us; we must save ourselves. (Principle 1, H.M. II)

Promises of immortal salvation or fear of eternal damnation are both illusory and harmful... There is no credible evidence that life survives the death of the body. (Principle 2, H.M.II)

We affirm that moral values derive their source from human experience. Ethics is autonomous and situational, needing no theological or ideological sanction. Ethics stems from human need and interest. To deny this distorts the whole basis of life. Human life has meaning because we create and develop our futures. (Principles 3, H.M.II)

Reason and intelligence are the most effective instruments that humankind possesses. There is no substitute: neither faith nor passion suffices in itself. The controlled use of scientific methods, which have transformed the natural and social sciences since the Renaissance, must be extended further in the solution of human problems. (Principle 4, H.M.II) [66]

This is enough to give you an idea of what Humanism is all about. It is the ancient Greek religion of man as the measure of all things. Regrettably, many Americans have been converted to it, whether they realize it or not.

The realization that Humanism has gradually taken prominence over the former Judeo-Christian consensus in our schools, media, government, and law during the last fifty years has given rise to no small sense of alarm. The church is coming to the sober realization that America's biblical foundation may be totally swept away. The fruit of a privatized Christianity has nearly reached full term. The battle lines have been clearly drawn between two faiths in conflict. Faith in man versus faith in God, faith in reason versus faith in revelation, faith in the creation versus faith in the Creator.

This matter of not mixing religion with our schools today is an issue which needs to be carefully reexamined. The question is not whether or not religion will be allowed to mix with education, but which religion will be allowed to mix. The fact of the matter is, religion is being mixed with our public schools today. It's just a different religion than the one that mixed with education in our country from the colonial days until the 1960s.

Consider this: if it is not allowable to teach that the world was created by God, and yet it is allowable to teach that the world came into being on its own, is it not equally a religious position to teach that God did not create the world as it is to teach that He did? If it is a religious statement to say, "God created the world," is it not also a religious statement to say, "God did not create the world"? Are not both positions of faith?

To teach children that God did not create the world can be done very effectively without actually saying those specific words. A teacher does not have to stand up in front of a class full of students and tell them that the biblical account of creation is a myth in order to communicate the idea that it is.

Consider this: if it is not allowable to teach children that God has spoken to man through the Bible and that His Word is an absolute moral standard for man, and yet it is allowable to teach them that morality is something determined by society itself and is relative to society's own desires and ideals, then is it not an equally religious position to teach that God's Word is not the moral standard for man as it is to teach that it is? Are not both positions based on faith? If it is a religious statement to say, "The Bible is man's ultimate standard of morality," is it not also a religious statement to say, in so many words or lack thereof, "The Bible is not man's ultimate standard of morality"?

All schools are faith-based, just like all civil institutions and churches are. It can be no other way, for all ideologies are based on certain assumptions which can only be accepted by faith. It takes faith to believe that God created the world, and it takes faith to believe that the world evolved on its own. It takes faith to believe that the Bible is a book of moral absolutes, and it takes faith to believe that man is the measure of all things. It is impossible to divorce education, government, or any other sphere of life from faith assumptions of one sort or another. And furthermore, somebody's faith will end up being the guiding factor in any of these spheres of life, be it in the classroom or the pulpit, on the playground or in parliament.

Is the infiltration of humanistic religion into our schools a conspiracy? The fact of the matter is, a conspiracy is hardly necessary. Like an epidemic of measles, Humanism has infected every institution to one degree or another, both public and private. This spirit is an ancient one with real teeth, and it is not tolerant of other faiths. Having gained increasing momentum since the days of the Renaissance, Humanism is now running in high gear.

The similarities between Humanism and ancient Greek philosophy should be clear enough to anyone who has read this book with understanding up to this point. Paul Kurtz, professor of philosophy at the State University of New York, editor of Free Inquiry, and major contributor to the *Humanist*

*Manifesto II*, claimed: "Our model is not Moses, Jesus, or Mohammed, but Socrates." [67] Of this there can be little doubt or debate. Socrates' ancient model of using rationalism to determine moral truth became one of the hallmarks of Greek philosophy. With reason as the determining factor of right and wrong, revelation can be rejected with relative ease. This our current culture has done with vigorous abandon.

It has been said a man's morality will dictate his theology or his philosophy. When it comes to deciding how to act in life, a person will lean upon an inner set of assumptions for support in order to maintain a sense of mental stability. Since most people prefer mental stability over mental instability, either people will align their behavior with their inner belief system, or they will seek to change their belief system so that they can behave the way they want to without feeling a sense of guilt. Our culture has been on a fast track with the second option.

Many Americans, whose desires are in conflict with Scripture, have found in the ancient model of Socrates a welcomed and convenient means of justification for personal immorality. The "values clarification" movement in American education, which began in the 1960s, opened the floodgates. Now, after forty years of clarifying values, one thing is abundantly clear: our values are clearly in need of a radical change of direction. The similarities between decadent Greece and our current situation are sobering, and the fruit of present day Humanism is not looking very good at all.

William Bennett, in *The Index of Leading Cultural Indicators* (1994), pointed out that in the thirty years since 1960, violent crime in America increased more than 500 percent, illegitimate births increased by more than 400 percent, the percentage of children living with single parents tripled, as did the teenage suicide rate, while the divorce rate doubled. The prognosis by this former Secretary of Education and Director of the Office of National Drug Control Policy is stark and to the point: "Over the past three decades we have experienced substantial social regression. Today the forces of social decomposition are challenging, and in some instances, overtaking, the forces of social composition. And when decomposition takes hold, it extracts an enormous human cost. *Unless these exploding social pathologies are reversed, they will lead to the decline and perhaps even to the fall of the American republic.*" [68] [Emphasis by Bennett.]

Perhaps the model of Socrates is not the one we should be following after all. The Roman Empire could not survive with Greek assumptions, and neither will we. We should heed the admonition of the Roman historian Titus Livy (59 B.C. - A.D. 17), an eyewitness to Rome's decay, who penned the following in his *History of Rome:*

I would then have [the reader] trace the process of our moral decline, to watch, first, the sinking of the foundations of morality as the old teaching was allowed to lapse, then the rapidly increasing disintegration, then the final collapse of the whole edifice, and the dark dawning of our modern day when we can neither endure our vices nor face the remedies needed to cure them. The study of history is the best medicine for a sick mind; for in history you have a record of the infinite variety of human experience plainly set out for all to see; and in that record you can find for yourself and your country both examples and warnings; fine things to take as models, base things, rotten through and through, to avoid.[69]

## CHAPTER SIX SUMMARY: KEY PEOPLE, PLACES AND CONCEPTS
Puritans and Puritanism
Charles Darwin (1809-1882)
William James (1842-1910)
John Dewey (1859-1952)
American Humanist Association
*Humanist Manifestos*
Ideology
Deism
Natural law
Darwinism
Pragmatism
Progressive education
Nontheistic religion
Humanism
Rationalism
Values clarification
The Hebrew concept of wisdom

*For Further Thought and Discussion*

1. Explain why it is impossible to separate faith from education, or religion from schooling.

2. How has the theory of evolution infiltrated all spheres of modern thought and practice?

3. Give examples of how wisdom differs from intelligence.

4. Explain the meaning of this statement: "A man's morality will dictate his theology." How does this apply in our culture today?

5. Compare and contrast the role of education for the Hebrews, the Spartans, and the Athenians. What parallels are there with current educational practice in America?

6. For Christian parents who seek alternatives to the current public educational system for their children, what options do they have?

7. What do you think makes a Christian school "Christian?" How can Christian schools guard themselves from becoming as "Greek" as any other school?

8. If you were the principal of a private or public school, and you held to the biblical assumptions regarding education which you have read in this book, what steps would you take to:
   a) nurture a community of likeminded parents?
   b) build and insure a staff of likeminded teachers?

9. What hiring criteria would you have for teachers and staff?

10. What would you do to build an awareness in your student body that wisdom and virtue are more highly valued than academic accomplishment, sports, and/or music?

# Chapter Eight

# The Prevailing Wind of Postmodernism

W hile Humanism flourished in the 20th Century, the 21st Century brings even more compelling challenges. Like ancient Athenians in the 5th Century B.C., many people today have reached a point of pessimism and doubt about the idea that truth can be known at all. While some have come to the conclusion that truth is unknowable, others are suggesting it is "multidimensional." Welcome to the postmodern age.

We conclude our journey with the following excerpt from *Making the Connections*, a book by Christian Overman and Don Johnson written on the topic of putting biblical worldview integration into practice.*

For many people, the word "postmodern" seemed to come out of nowhere in the 90s and suddenly spread everywhere. Although historian Arnold Toynbee is said to have first coined the word 'Post-Modern' back in 1954, when he used it to describe Western civilization's decline into irrationality and relativism, the term didn't start to crystallize in the academic world until about the mid-1970s. Culture-watchers were still defining it in the 90s.

To understand the meaning of "postmodern," we'll start with the word "modern." This is because postmodernism is perhaps best understood as a reaction to modernism.

The roots of the modern era of Western civilization go back to the 17th century, to the scientific revolution. The discoveries of Copernicus, Kepler, Galileo and Newton opened new perspectives on the world, and birthed different ways of thinking. By the time of the Enlightenment, in the 18th century, modernism was in high gear.

---

* Excerpt from *Making the Connections* by Christian Overman and Don Johnson. Copyright 2002 by The Biblical Worldview Institute, a division of Cascade Christian Schools, 815 21st Street SE, Puyallup, WA 98372. 253.841.1776, www.biblicalworldviewinstitute.org. Reprinted by permission.

The very word "enlightenment" connotes the notion that a new light had dawned upon the West. This new "light" was the light of human reason. However, it was not just any sort of reason, it was an "objective" reason, that is, reason independent of revelation or supernatural input. It was a kind of reason that was based solely upon that which could be proven through scientific discovery and empirical evidence.

With the Enlightenment, a new approach to determining truth and reality emerged. Truth was no longer to be discovered by looking to revelation from God, or to church councils, but rather by means of scientific observation and measurement. The five senses of sight, touch, taste, sound and smell governed one's concept of what was really real and true. In this approach to knowledge, scientific rationalism became the new guiding light. God, miracles and the supernatural were relegated to the realm of folklore.

During the modern era, optimism steadily grew with the belief that science and the scientific method would eventually solve all problems known to man. "Progress" through human intelligence and scientific rationalism energized Western civilization. Modernity had arrived, and with it the hope of a utopian society.

Along with the elevating of objective human reason and the rejection of the supernatural, came a belief that mankind was the ultimate center of meaning and significance. A man-centered, materialist, rationalist view of the world emerged and grew.

Modernity also brought with it the idea that mankind could discover universal truths – truths that applied to everyone – through human reason and the scientific method. These overarching, objective truths would define what was really good, what was really evil, what was really right and what was really wrong – not only for individuals, but for whole societies. This belief was, in part, the result of approaching social issues with the same kind of scientific methodology with which one might approach chemicals and numbers.

**THE TIDE TURNS**

The later part of the twentieth century saw the optimism of modernity turn into postmodern cynicism. Some scholars see the 1960s as a pivotal decade between the modern era and the postmodern era. By the 1990s, modernism was in serious crisis. After two hundred years of trust in human autonomy, elevating reason and devaluing divine revelation, the twentieth century brought wars of unthinkable proportion, nuclear bombs, bloodshed of a magnitude never imagined, and ideological conflicts beyond belief. Science and the scientific method began to be viewed with suspicion – if not downright rejected. If this was "progress," who needed it? If reason based upon the scientific method brought us to the brink of self-destruction, perhaps it wasn't such a trustworthy light after all.

The old modern idea that universal truth can be discovered by means of scientific rationalism is no longer held in postmodernism. In fact, the very notion of "objective" reason itself has come under fire. Some postmodern thinkers deny that human beings are capable of being truly objective. Their rationale is that any criterion a human being may come up with for determining "objective" truth is, in itself, the subjective product of a human mind and, therefore, of human language. And because human language is culturally conditioned and socially influenced, it raises postmodern suspicions about any claims to the "universality" of any particular truth.

Postmodernists assert that truth that is universally true for everybody does not exist. This is because they see truth as something that is determined differently by different groups [or "tribes"] in different social and cultural contexts. This communal relativism produces such statements as, "What is true [or, 'right'] for us, may not be true for you." It has also allowed non-Christians to express ideas to Christians like, "I'm glad you've found the truth – for you! If it works for you, great!" The same person may hold to atheism as "truth for them." Truth, for the postmodernist, has become a matter of preference. The fact that a concept of truth held by one group contradicts what is "true" for another group, is not a serious problem. While empirical, scientifically proven evidence stood in judgment over all claims of truth or reality in the modern era, in the postmodern era, culture and social perspectives are taken much more seriously.

If this line of thinking is carried to its logical conclusion, Buddhism and Christianity may be seen as contradicting each other, yet both may be viewed as true within the context of the cultures that hold them as such. They are both products of human societies, postmodernism claims. If this is indeed the case, then who is to say one group's concept of reality is true and another is false? For one group to claim they have the only truth is viewed as repressive today.

If all religions and ideologies are equally true, then it is not permitted for one to say that another religion or ideology is false. The cardinal sin of postmodernism is for one group to be intolerant of another group's values or ethics.

However, to be "tolerant" today not only means that one *allows* others to believe and practice their own concepts of truth, but that one *accepts* the fact that any other group's concept of truth is just as true as yours! After all, if truth is a social construct, expressed through language having culturally conditioned meanings, then it is not only beauty that is in the eye of the beholder, but truth as well. There are no "absolute" truths, according to postmodernism, and absolutes can neither be found through reason nor revelation.

Along with the postmodern reaction to the idea of scientifically determining truth via reason has come the postmodern acceptance of intuition or "gut instinct" as a valid factor in determining what is true. While Christians can be thankful that many postmodern people are open to the idea that there are other ways of knowing truth besides through human reason and the scientific method, turning to human intuition and inner feelings is just as problematic. Does believing that a certain idea is true make it true? Can truth be humanly determined? Is there no objective standard of truth by which the truth claims of every society and culture must be measured?

## A DIFFERENT CENTER

In the postmodern era, a new "celebration of diversity" and "multiculturalism" has brought with it the idea that there is no objective standard. The notion that non-European cultures and ideas have been intolerantly devalued in the West has become a major focus of growing grievance. Included in this grievance is the claim that traditional Christianity itself is oppressive and victimizing. Oppressive in that it does not tolerate [accept] others' view of what is right or wrong, and victimizing in that it "discriminates" against groups with differing views of right and wrong. To say biblical precepts apply to everyone is now viewed as intolerant arrogance.

In the pre-modern era of Western civilization [during the Middle Ages], the center of meaning for mankind was ultimately found in the supernatural God and His will on earth. In the modern era, the center of meaning shifted from God to man. In postmodernism, however, there is no standard center of meaning, other than that which a particular group determines to be the "center" of meaning for them. While the center of meaning for a Christian mission agency may be God, the center of meaning for an extreme environmentalist group may be "Nature."

**WHAT IS REALLY REAL?**

For some postmodernists, reality itself is a human construct. If this is the case, we live in a vast realm of multiple realities. In the 1960s the cry of the hour was, "Question authority – let's be our own!" But by the 1990s, the cry of the hour, for many, had become, "Question reality – let's construct our own!" The theme of questioning reality is seen in such popular films as The Truman Show and The Matrix. The idea of constructing reality is heard from such New Age gurus as Deepak Chopra and Shirley MacLaine.

The West is currently experiencing a resurgence of an age-old question: "What is really real?" It is the same question that drove the ancient Greeks through 200 years of philosophic speculation after Thales of Ionia declared the sun and the stars to be "balls of fire" and not gods after all, nearly 600 years before Christ. Whether this reemergence of the questioning of reality is the outcome of a postmodern reaction to modernism, or the result of the hyper-individualism of the 1970s, or the embracing of Eastern Religions, or a mixture of all of the above, is open to discussion. But the fact is it is part of the current sea of surrounding ideas our youth are swimming in today.

Yet it is not just youth that are surrounded. Even in such high places as the United States Supreme Court, the right to shape one's own concept of reality is touted as a basic tenet of freedom. Consider this definition of liberty from the joint opinion of Justices O'Connor, Kennedy and Souter, in Planned Parenthood v. Casey, 1992: "At the heart of liberty is the right to define one's own concept of existence, of meaning, of the universe, and of the mystery of human life."

Carrying such a "construct-your-own-concept-of-existence" to its logical conclusion is a chilling prospect indeed. Not only could such a concept of liberty be used to justify abortion, but infanticide as well. In fact, it already has. So-called 'partial birth abortion,' legalized by the Supreme Court in the year 2000, is nothing short of infanticide. And if infanticide can be legalized, why not genocide?

For reasons such as these, we believe the consequences of failing to integrate the unchanging and enduring biblical worldview into the minds of the next generation are enormously serious, both for individuals as well as the entire culture. Furthermore, if there ever was a time to articulate the basics of the biblical worldview to the next generation, and to demonstrate how this worldview connects with all of reality, it is now.

This is our hour of opportunity, both in Christian and public schools.

## SOME POSITIVE ASPECTS

While the "death of universal truth" is indeed a bleak outcome of the demise of modernism, the dawning of postmodernism brings with it a new window of possibilities for Christians. The decline of modernism, with its rejection of the supernatural and its idolatrous worship of human reason, is a turn of events for which Christians must be thankful. Yes, postmodernism has brought with it some things for which we can rejoice! The rejection of human reason and the scientific method as ultimate measurements of reality is a welcome relief. People are more open to the idea of the supernatural, and are willing to take it seriously. The concept of life after death is receiving renewed attention. While this has given rise to popular radio and television shows dealing with the "paranormal," and to an acceptance of Eastern ideas like reincarnation, a new opportunity for Christians to speak the biblical worldview into the marketplace of postmodern ideas is now upon us.

Is modernism dead? Not by a long shot! Both modernism and postmodernism are forces we deal with every day. This is the world in which our children are growing up. It is a world for which they must be prepared, and they must be equipped to face serious ideological challenges on both fronts.

Is postmodernism a worldview? Not really. We prefer to think of it as a "prevailing wind" rather than a specific worldview. It is a "climate" which allows certain worldviews to flourish. Just as the prevailing wind of modernism during the early years of the twentieth century allowed atheistic worldviews such as Marxism and Humanism to flourish, postmodernism has opened the door for pantheistic worldviews, such as New Age and various Eastern religions, to find new acceptance in the West.

A person's worldview matters! And because it does, it is important for Christian youth to: 1) clearly comprehend the distinctiveness of the biblical worldview; 2) fully understand how the biblical worldview connects with every aspect of the world around us; and 3) know why the biblical worldview makes more sense than any other worldview out there.

No people are in a more strategic position to accomplish these key objectives than parents, pastors and educators. Working together, we can form a "three-fold cord" that will not be easily be broken. And work together we must, for such a time as this.

**CHAPTER SEVEN SUMMARY: KEY PEOPLE, PLACES AND CONCEPTS**

Postmodernism

Modernism

The Scientific Revolution

Universal Truth

Absolutes

Social construct

Tolerance

*For Further Thought and Discussion*

1. What postmodern influences have you personally noticed in the media? in contemporary film? in the church? in politics?

2. What effect do you think postmodern thought may have in the area of interpretation of Scripture?

3. According to research by Josh McDowell, 65% of Christian young people "either believe or suspect there's no way to tell which religion is true." McDowell further found that 48% suspect "it does not matter what religious faith you follow because all faiths teach similar lessons." [*The Disconnected Generation*, Word Publishing, 2000, p. 214.] McDowell believes such ideas are indicative of postmodern influences. If a young person made such statements to you, what words or key concepts would you choose to use in response?

Epilogue

# Where Do We Go
# From Here?

A n epilogue was a short speech presented directly to the audience by one of the actors following the final scene of an ancient play. It was not part of the play but a concluding statement. We have come to the end of this book and I wish now to bring some final thoughts to the reader.

I am reminded of a Friday night in a small church near Bellingham, Washington. My theme was the special uniqueness of a biblical worldview and how it greatly differs from the pagan views surrounding us today. I explained why our culture is in such deep trouble, and warned that unless we make a great turn in our course, we will end up in the same place decadent Greece did, or worse. However, I encouraged the group with the hope that such a turn was possible and shared how it could come about.

It was afterward that a young man came up to me with this sincere question: "Do you know of any culture that has made the turn?" Strangely enough, I hadn't given this important question much thought before. It was obvious from the look on his face that he hoped to hear an encouraging, "Yes," in reply, and with all my heart I wanted to give him the answer he wanted to hear. But his countenance fell dramatically when I replied, "No. I don't."

I went to bed troubled that night. I was disturbed because I didn't have a better answer for this man. What he wanted was hope. The kind of hope that comes from the realization that if others can make the turn, maybe we can too. But when I woke the next morning, it suddenly dawned on me that I had completely overlooked the obvious. My mind went back to the ancient days of Israel and Judah, and I began to realize that the answer to this man's question was found, once again, in the Hebrew model itself.

The history of ancient Israel is one of drifting away from God, and turning back again. The fact that they drifted away from God so much should not surprise us. The propensity of man to go his own way is awfully compelling. Since no man is exempt from this tendency, no group of people is exempt.

When it comes to drifting away, the model of the Hebrews is stark and chilling. At one point, they went so far as to offer their children as human sacrifices (Jeremiah 19:5). This in itself should give us hope that our own situation is not beyond remedy. But it is also a sober reminder that while turning back to God is always possible, keeping it that way is never guaranteed by one generation for the next.

The story of Ezra and Nehemiah is one of the bright spots in Hebrew history. Here we see Nehemiah rebuilding the walls of Jerusalem, and Ezra restoring the Word of God to the consciousness of the people. The sobering thing is, this turning back to God had to be preceded by seventy years of captivity in Babylon. The question is, will America's turn happen before greater judgment, or after it? Without doubt our judgment is already in progress, but for our children's sake, I pray even more severe judgment will not be necessary. It doesn't have to be that way. Certainly this is not God's first choice for us. We must be encouraged with the understanding that with God all things are possible, and nothing is too difficult for Him. Not even a secularized America.

One day a newsletter came across my desk. The opening paragraphs caught my attention, because they spoke so plainly to our situation:

When Alexander Solzhenitsyn sought an explanation for the devastating revolution that destroyed his native Russia, he recalled what those who had lived through the Bolshevik takeover had said: "Men have forgotten God, that's why all these things happened." Solzhenitsyn admitted that after decades of study he could not offer a better explanation. Historians say that those who do not learn from history are condemned to repeat its mistakes. Solzhenitsyn's conclusion is certainly a lesson to heed: when men forget God, some very terrible things happen. Leadership becomes corrupt. Marriages end. Families suffer. Churches split. Communities decay. Eventually, an entire nation crumbles.[70]

These words are true. Russia's seventy years were dark and painful. But, thankfully, the flip side is also true: when men remember God, some very wonderful things happen! Leadership becomes trustworthy once again. Marriages are solid. Families are a joy. Churches are strong. Communities flourish. Eventually, an entire nation is restored. Yes, pity the nation whose God was once the Lord. But rejoice with the nation who turns once again to Him.

"Remembering God," however, is not something superficial. In my opinion, long term, significant national change for America requires a broad-based, deep-rooted change at the assumption level of our citizenry at large. This is how we got into our present condition, and this is how we will get out. What made America so remarkable in the past is not just that our laws and institutions were Bible-based, or even that many of our political and social leaders were Christians. As important as these things were, they were only half of the equation. The other half was this: most people, throughout all walks of life, whether Christians or not, generally held to Judeo-Christian assumptions.

Even in those days, this stood in sharp contrast to other nations which were adversely affected by Greek philosophy, such as France, the seat of the so-called Enlightenment. That the American people held to much different views can be seen in these candid remarks by Ben Franklin, which he made to the French:

Bad examples to youth are more rare in America, which must be a comfortable consideration to parents. To this may be truly added, that serious religion, under its various denominations, is not only tolerated, but respected and practiced. Atheism is unknown there; infidelity rare and secret; so that persons may live to a great age in that country without having their piety shocked by meeting with either an Atheist or an Infidel.[71]

As Christians, we must be politically active, for sure. We must take our place in the arenas of legislative, judicial, and executive responsibility, just as we once did years ago. But this is not the complete answer. Laws will not change the hearts of our people. Nor will political reform. We must pray for God to do a work on the inside of people. We must pray they will come to personally know the God of Abraham, Isaac, and Jacob, and align their assumptions with His Holy Word, out of a love relationship with Him through Jesus Christ. We need a spiritual awakening which no law can produce. The much needed moral changes will naturally follow.

This is not to say Christians should wait for such an awakening before they take responsible action in what they know to do. By God's grace we must do a better job of loving our spouses; fathers must turn their hearts to their children and take an active role in shaping the moral character of the next generation; we must teach our children to honor and respect God and others, and put virtue back into the educational curriculum, whether in public or private settings; we must support our local churches, helping them to be strong and effective in equipping the saints for the work of service; we must do our labor as unto the Lord, be it preaching or plumbing, recognizing that when done unto Him, all work is worship; we must take part in civil responsibilities; and we must acknowledge that the Kingdom of God is a reality in whatever part of His field we're planted, understanding that the world and all it contains belongs to Him. In short, we must occupy until He comes again.

# Appendix

Listed below are twenty-four major distinctions between Greek and Hebrew thought.

1. **Greek:** Mother Earth is the impersonal source of all life on the planet.

   **Hebrew:** Father God is the personal source of all life on planet Earth as well as the planet itself and all things beyond.

2. **Greek:** Nature is a self-generating force, operating according to its own closed system of laws and acting independently of any authority outside of itself.

   **Hebrew:** Creation is generated by the Creator-God who made it for His purposes, operating according to laws designed and sustained by Him and subject to His authority. While the Greek sees laws of Nature, the Hebrew sees laws over nature.

3. **Greek:** Nature is "God" and "God" is Nature. All that is, is natural. The supernatural simply does not exist. [Ionian thought.]

   **Hebrew:** Creation is God's handiwork. God is not to be confused with what He has made, for He existed prior to and is distinct from that which He created. He is a supernatural being, inhabiting the supernatural as well as the natural, created world.

4. **Greek:** The Olympian gods are personal yet limited, while Nature is unlimited yet impersonal.

   **Hebrew:** The God of Abraham, Issac, and Jacob is unlimited yet personal.

5. **Greek:** The gods are created in the image and likeness of man.

   **Hebrew:** Man is created in the image and likeness of God.

6. **Greek:** Man is classified as an animal, distinguished by this specific difference: man is a rational animal. [Aristotle.]

   **Hebrew:** Man is differentiated from animals and unique from all other living things in that he is the only creature made in the likeness and image of God.

7. **Greek:** Man's appearance on earth is the result of an impersonal, non-rational act of a force called "Nature." No purpose is involved. No meaning for existence is given. Mother Nature is silent.

   **Hebrew:** Man's appearance on earth is premeditated by a personal, rational Being, and is a deliberate and decisive act of intelligence with purpose.

8. **Greek:** Mankind has no mandate from any source above man himself.

   **Hebrew:** Man's divine mandate is to care for creation, and to rule responsibly over the earth.

9. **Greek:** Man's value and worth is determined by the society into which he is born.

   **Hebrew:** Man has intrinsic value because he is created in the image and likeness of God. He has God-determined worth, independent of society's opinion.

10. **Greek:** Truth is measured by man's intellect and reasoned judgment. There is no divine standard or measure of truth which stands over and above man's determination of it. "Man is the measure of all things."

    **Hebrew:** Truth is determined by God, independently of man. God's Word is the measure of all things. Man's opinion does not affect it in any way.

11. **Greek:** The faith of Greek philosophers is built upon reason acting independently of divine revelation.

    **Hebrew:** The faith of the Hebrews is built upon revelation from God, to which human reason submits.

12. **Greek:** Religious expression is centered around rituals such as food offerings to gods and other rites. Correct ritual receives more emphasis than conduct. The gods do not speak to such issues as business, law, relationships, labor, or family.

    **Hebrew:** Religious expression is a commitment to a way of life. God is as relevant to behavior on the Sabbath as He is to what is done during the rest of the week. His Word speaks to all spheres of life, be it business, law, relationships, labor, or family.

13. **Greek:** Religion is a personal choice, a private matter. There are many gods to worship and creeds to choose in Athens.

    **Hebrew:** God and His Word are not dependent upon human acceptance or rejection. His reality and man's accountability to this reality stand, regardless of human consent.

14. **Greek:** Moral conduct is relative to public opinion and/or individual conscience. The Greeks had no Bible to regulate thought and conduct. Values are relative to the social environment.

    **Hebrew:** Moral conduct is relative only to God's Word, and in this respect it is absolute. Public opinion and individual conscience have no power to alter what God has declared true or morally right.

15. Greek: For the citizen of Athens, to "show himself the rightful lord and owner of his own person in all the manifold aspects of life" is an exalted right. [Pericles.]

    Hebrew: For the Hebrew, to show himself the rightful and obedient servant of God his maker and owner is his joyful blessing, privilege, and obligation.

16. Greek: Human freedom is self-determined.

    Hebrew: Human freedom is God-determined.

17. Greek: Wisdom is found from within.

    Hebrew: Wisdom is found from without. Foolishness is found within.

18. Greek: "Know thyself." [Socrates.]

    Hebrew: Know God.

19. Greek: "The Greeks learned in order to comprehend..."

    Hebrew: "The Hebrews learned in order to revere." [Abraham Heschel.]

20. Greek: "The Greek asked, 'Why must I do it?'"

    Hebrew: "The Hebrew asked, 'What must I do?'" [Abraham Heschel.]

21. Greek: In Sparta, education is for "the obliteration of the individual in the service of the state." In Athens, it is for "the training of the individual in the service of culture."

    Hebrew: In Israel, education is for "the training of the individual in the service of God." [William Barclay.]

22. Greek: Manual labor is viewed by philosophers as vulgar and beneath a citizen's dignity.

    Hebrew: Trades are honored and manual labor is respected so much that rabbis are expected to be proficient in a trade as well as the Law.

23. Greek: Old age is feared.

    Hebrew: Old age is honored.

24. Greek: History is viewed as a cycle of aimless repetition. The same basic pattern of life and death goes on with no particular end or destination in sight.

    Hebrew: History is viewed as going somewhere, like an arrow to its target. Theirs is a straight-line concept of history, with God working His purposes in the earth, culminating in the messianic reign of Israel's Redeemer.

# Recommended Reading

(** = a "must read" book)

Barton, David. *The Myth of Separation*. Aledo, Texas: Wallbuilder Press, 1992.

Beckett, John. *Loving Monday*. InterVarsity Press, 1998.

Bennett, William J. *The Index of Leading Cultural Indicators*. New York, Simon and Schuster, 1994.

Blamires, Harry. *The Christian Mind: How Should A Christian Think?* Ann Arbor, Michigan, Servant Books, 1963.

Blankenhorn, David. *Fatherless America*. Basic Books, 1995. [**] A clear and convincing book about the loss of the idea of "fatherhood" in our culture and the negative results of this loss in society.

Boman, Thorlief. *Hebrew Thought Compared with Greek*. New York, New York: W.W. Norton and Co., Inc., 1960.

Briner, Bob. *Roaring Lambs*. Zondervan, 1993.[**]

Brown, Colin. *Philosophy and the Christian Faith*. Downers Grove, Illinois: InterVarsity Press, 1968.

Brown, Willliam, and Phillips, Gary. *Making Sense of Your World*. Sheffield Publishing, 1996.

Byrne, H. W. *A Christian Approach to Education*. Milsord, Mississippi: Mott Media, 1977.

Cornford, Francis MacDonald. *Before and After Socrates*. Cambridge University Press, 1932. Cornford was a professor at Cambridge, with a very high regard for Greek thought. This book discusses the Ionian Science of Nature, which first disregarded the supernatural and claimed all that "is," is "natural."

Colson, Charles, and Pearcey, Nancy. *How Now Shall We Live?* Tyndale House, 1999. [**]

DeMar, Gary. *God and Government: A Biblical and Historical Study*. Brentwood, Tennessee, Wolgemuth and Hyatt, 1984.

Durant, Will. *The Life of Greece*. New York: Simon and Schuster, 1939.

Edersheim, Alfred. *Sketches of Jewish Social Life in the Days of Christ*. Grand Rapids, Michigan: Wm. B. Eerdmans Publishing Co., reprinted 1982. An excellent description of ancient Hebraic culture, written in a reader-friendly style.

Ezzo, Gary and Anne Marie. *Growing Kids God's Way*. Growing Families International, 2130 Cheswick Lane, Mount Pleasant, SC 29466 [**] Video series and workbook. Ethics for parenting.

Freeman, James M. *Manners and Customs of the Bible*. Plainfield, New Jersey: Logos International, 1972. A very helpful resource in understanding the differences between our current culture and the culture of the ancient Hebrews as it is expressed in the Bible.

Fugate, Richard. *What the Bible Says about Child Training*. Garland, Texas: Alethera Publishers, Inc., 1980. An especially good book for parents on how to "bend the twig" the right way at an early age.

Gaebelein, Frank E. *The Pattern of God's Truth: The Integration of Faith and Learning*. Chicago, Moody Press, 1954. A classic.

Greene, Albert. *Ten Touchstones to Distinctively Christian Thought*. Alta Vista College, P.O. Box 222, Medina, WA 98039.

Hitchcock, James. *What is Secular Humanism?: Why Humanism Became Secular and How it is Changing Our World*. Ann Arbor, Michigan, Servant Books, 1982.

Holmes, Arthur F. *All Truth is God's Truth*. Grand Rapids, Michigan: Wm. B. Eerdmans Publishing Co., 1977.

Johnson, Paul. *Modern Times*. New York, Harper and Row, 1983.

Jones, E. Stanley. *The Unshakable Kingdom and the Unchanging Person*. Nashville, Abingdon Press, 1972. [**]

Knight, George, R. *Philosophy and Education: An Introduction in Christian Perspective*. Berrien Springs, Michigan, Andrews University Press, 1980. A very well written, clear introduction to the topic.

Lee, Francis Nigel. *A Christian Introduction to the History of Philosophy*. Nutley, New Jersey: The Craig Press, 1969.

McCallum, Dennis, ed. *The Death of Truth*. Bethany House Publishers, 1996.

McDowell, Josh. *The Disconnected Generation*. Word Publishing, 2000.

Miller, Darrow. *Discipling Nations*. YWAM Publishing, 1998.

Morris, Henry. *The Long War Against God*. Baker Book House, Grand Rapids, Michigan, 1989. [**] This is by far the best book I have read on the long-range negative effects of evolutionism in all fields of thought and practice.

Noebel, David. *The Battle For Truth*. Harvest House Publishers, 2001.

Ryken, Leland. *Worldly Saints: The Puritans As They Really Were*. Grand Rapids: Zondervan Publishing House, 1986.

Schaeffer, Francis. *How Should We Then Live?* Old Tappan, New Jersey: Fleming H. Revell, 1976. [**] Just about anything written by Francis Schaeffer is worth reading, but this book is especially good at tracing the history of Western thought from the time of Rome to the present.

Schaeffer, Francis. *The Great Evangelical Disaster.* Westchester, Ill., Crossway Books, 1984.

Singer, C. Gregg. *A Theological Interpretation of American History.* Phillipsburg, New Jersey, Presbyterian and Reformed Publishing Co., 1964.

Sire, James. *The Universe Next Door.* InterVarsity Press, 1997.

Smith, Gary Scott, ed. *God and Politics: Four Views on the Reformation of Civil Government.* Phillipsburg, New Jersey, Presbyterian and Reformed Publishing Co., 1989. This book will cause you to think about what it means (and doesn't mean) for Christians to be involved in civil government. Four differing viewpoints are presented – you can draw your own conclusions.

Steensma, Geraldine and Van Brummelen, Harro. *Shaping School Curriculum: A Biblical View.* Terre Haute, Indiana: Signal 8 Publishing Co., 1977.

Storkey, Alan. *A Christian School Perspective.* Leicester, England: Inter-Varsity Press, 1979.

Veith, Eugene, Edward. *Postmodern Times.* Crossway Books, 1994.

Walsh, Brian J., and Middleton, J. Richard. *The Transforming Vision: Shaping a Christian World View.* Downers Grove, Ill., InterVarsity Press, 1984.

Whitehead, John. *The Second American Revolution.* Crossway Books, Wheaton, Ill., 1985. [**] This book is especially good on dealing with the current problems of our justice system being built upon relativistic thinking. Clearly written by a lawyer.

Wilson, Marvin R. *Our Father Abraham: Jewish Roots of the Christian Faith.* Grand Rapids, Michigan: William B. Eerdmans Publishing Company, 1989. [**] Marvin Wilson is the best authority on this subject I know. Also very reader-friendly.

Wolters, Albert M. *Creation Regained: Biblical Basics for a Reformational Worldview.* Grand Rapids, Michigan, Eerdmans Publishing Co., 1985. [**] A short book, summarizing the basics of a biblical worldview.

# Endnotes

1. Will Durant, *The Life of Greece* (New York: Simon and Schuster, 1939), 565-568.

2. *Time,* 28 May 1973, 104.

3. Durant, 287.

4. C. Bakewell, *Source Book in Ancient Philosophy,* (New York: Scribner's, 1907), 6.

5. Quoted in Richard Hertz, *Chance and Symbol* (Chicago: University of Chicago Press, 1948), 107.

6. *Plutarch's Lives,* Vol. 1 (Boston: Little, Brown, 1905), 115.

7. Ibid., 117.

8. J. E. Dobson, *Ancient Education and Its Meaning to Us* (New York: Longmans, Green, 1932), 5.

9. Immanuel Jakobovits, "Jewish Views on Abortion," in *The Zero People,* ed. Jeff Lane Hensley (Ann Arbor, Mich.: Servant Books, 1983), 269.

10. Morris Frank and Blake Clark, *First Lady of the Seeing Eye,* (Holt, Rinehart and Winston, New York), 1957, 39-40.

11. Albert Greene, Jr., *Ten Touchstones of Distinctly Christian Thought,* 3, 10. (Alta Vista College, Medina, Washington.)

12. Plato, *Republic,* 457b-466d, (London: Oxford University Press, 1941), 159.

13. October 7, 1933. N.H. Baynes, ed., *The Speeches of Adolf Hitler, 1922-1939,* Vol. I, (London: Oxford University Press, 1942), 872.

14. William L. Shirer, *The Rise and Fall of the Third Reich* (New York: Simon and Schuster, 1960), 253-255.

15. Fredric Wertham, *A Sign for Cain* (New York: Macmillan, 1966), 180.

16. *Pediatrics,* Vol. 72, 1983, 128.

17. Plutarch, *Moralia,* English translation by Frank Cole Babbitt, (G.P. Putnam's Sons, New York, 1931), Vol. 3, 93 ["Sayings of Kings and Commanders," 185-10].

18. Paul Johnson, *Modern Times* (New York: Harper and Row, 1983), 18-19.

19. Arthur G. Powell, Eleanor Farrar, and David K. Cohen, *The Shopping Mall High School* (Boston: Houghton Mifflin Company, 1985), 40. Excerpts from *The Shopping Mall High School.* Copyright © 1985 by Arthur G. Powell, Eleanor Farrar and David K. Cohen. Reprinted by permission of Houghton Mifflin Co. All rights reserved.

20. Hayim Halevy Donin, *To Raise a Jewish Child* (New York: Basic Books, 1977), 77.

21. The dividing line between philosophy and religion may get blurred when the precepts of a particular philosophy seem to take on the role of revelation itself. In such cases, philosophy becomes religion. A modern example is Secular Humanism, which even the Supreme Court has called a religion.

22. Abram L. Sachar, *A History of the Jews* (New York: Alfred A. Knopf, 1948), 100.

23. Abraham Heschel, *The Insecurity of Freedom* (New York: Farrar, Strauss and Giroux, 1966), 41.

24. Marvin R. Wilson, *Our Father Abraham: Jewish Roots of the Christian Faith*, (Grand Rapids, Michigan: William B. Eerdmans Publishing Company, 1989), 171.

25. Francis Cornford, *Before and After Socrates*, (Cambridge University Press, 1972), 65.

26. Alexander Roberts and James Donaldson, eds., *The Ante-Nicene Fathers*, Vol. 1 (Grand Rapids: Eerdmans, 1981), 178.

27. Ibid., Vol. 2, 489.

28. Werner Jaeger, "The Greek Ideas of Immortality," Harvard Theological Review 52 (July, 1959): 146.

29. Pastor Richard Vicknair's response to a newspaper reporter, when asked for his reaction to members of the University Congregational Church in Seattle, Washington, calling a homosexual pair to share an associate pastorship. This is believed to be the first such invitation by an historic denominational church in American history. The decision was by a 76% majority vote of the congregation. (*The Seattle Times*, June 13, 1994.)

30. Archibald A. Hodge, *Evangelical Theology*, Carlisle, PA: (The Banner of Truth Trust, 1873, 1977), 280-281.

31. "Psychologist sues after losing license for praying with patient," Evangelical Press Service, *Northwest Christian Journal*, November, 1994.

32. As Martin Luther King, Jr., once said, "It may be true that the law cannot make a man love me. But it can keep him from lynching me, and I think that's pretty important." (Cindy Hall, "Martin Luther King, Jr.: 'Riots Are Voices of the Unheard,'" Gannett News Service, May 8, 1992.) [Now, if only the pre-born could speak.]

33. Donald S. Lutz, "The Relative Influence of European Writers on Late Eighteenth-Century American Political Thought," *The American Political Science Review*, Vol. 78, No. 1, March, 1984, 189-197. The following excerpt is especially noteworthy:

"If we ask what book was most frequently cited by Americans during the founding era, the answer somewhat surprisingly is: the book of Deuteronomy. The biblical tradition is most prominent among the citations. Since our concern in this essay is with sorting out the relative influence of European thinkers, the problem of how to count biblical citations is not important. It is relevant, nonetheless, to note the prominence of biblical sources for American political thought, since it was highly influential in our political tradition and is not always given the attention it deserves." [p. 192.]

34. Alexis de Tocqueville, *Democracy in America*, Henry Reeves, trans. (New York, NY: George Dearborn & Co., 1838), 281-291.

35. James D. Richardson, *A Compilation of the Messages and Papers of the Presidents, 1789-1897* (Published by the authority of Congress, 1899), Vol. 1, 220.

36. John Adams, *The Works of John Adams, Second President of the United States*, Charles Francis Adams, ed. (Boston: Little Brown, 1854), Vol. IX 229, Oct. 11, 1798.

37. Woodrow Wilson, *The Papers of Woodrow Wilson*, Vol. 23, (Princeton University Press, 1977), 18, 20. Following this speech, given to 12,000 people on May 7, 1911, Wilson wrote a personal note to a friend, Mary Ellen Hulbert Peck, in which he said: "The Bible... is undoubtedly the book that has made democracy and been the source of all progress." [Papers, 11]

38. *Imprimis*, the monthly journal of Hillsdale College, Hillsdale, Michigan, April, 1981.

39. Richardson, Vol. I, September 17, 1796, 220.

40. Abraham Lincoln, *The Collected Works of Abraham Lincoln*, Roy P. Basler, ed. (New Brunswick, NJ: Rutgers University Press, 1953), Vol. VII, September 7, 1864, 542.

41. Daniel Webster, *The Works of Daniel Webster*, (Boston: Charles C. Little and James Brown), 1851, Vol. I, 44.

42. Benjamin Franklin, *The Works of Benjamin Franklin*, John Bigelow, ed., (New York: G. P. Putnam's Sons), 1904, Vol. XI, April 17, 1787, 318.

43. Robert C. Winthrop, *Addresses and Speeches on Various Occasions*, (Boston: Little Brown and Co., 1852) 172.

44. Calvin Coolidge, *The Price of Freedom: Speeches and Addresses by Calvin Coolidge*, (New York: Charles Scribner's Sons, 1927), 290-291.

45. B.F. Morris, *The Christian Life and Character of the Civil Institutions of the United States* (Philadelphia: George W. Childs, 1864), 320-321.

46. Morris, 328.

47. Church of the Holy Trinity v. U.S., 143 U.S. 457 (1892)

48. David Barton, *The Myth of Separation*. (Aledo, Texas: Wallbuilder Press, 1992) 13. The author is indebted to David Barton for much of the information and inspiration for this chapter.

49. Everson v. Board of Education, 330 U.S. 1 (1947) at 18.

50. Alexis de Tocqueville, *Democracy in America*, Henry Reeves, trans. (New York, NY: George Dearborn & Co. 1838), 290.

51. Noah Webster, *The American Magazine*, (March, 1788), 215.

52. Harry R. Warfel, ed., *Letters of Noah Webster* (New York: Library Publishers, 1953), 453-57.

53. William Barclay, *Train up a Child* (Philadelphia: Westminster, 1959), 11, 49, 78.

54. Abraham J. Heschel, *God in Search of Man* (New York: Harper and Row, 1955), 75.

55. Abraham J. Heschel, *The Insecurity of Freedom* (New York: Schocken Books, 1972), 54-55.

56. Marvin R. Wilson, "The Jewish Concept of Learning: A Christian Appreciation," *Christian Scholar's Review*, 5, No. 4, 1976, 357. Copyright © 1976 by *Christian Scholar's Review*; reprinted by permission.

57. Leland Ryken, *Worldly Saints: The Puritans as They Really Were* (Grand Rapids: Zondervan Publishing House, 1986), 2.

58. John Milton, *Of Education*.

59. Ibid.

60. Ryken, 15, quoting from George Swinnock, *The Christian Man's Calling*.

61. David A. Lockmiller, *Scholars on Parade: Colleges, Universities, Costumes, and Degrees* (Toronto: Macmillan, 1969), 70.

62. Paul W. Shafer and John Howland Snow, *The Turning of the Tides* (New Canaan, Connecticut: The Long House, Inc., 1962), 1-3.

63. *John Dewey on Education: Selected Writings* (New York: Random House, 1964), 439.

64. John Dewey, *A Common Faith* (New Haven: Yale University Press, 1934), 87.

65. The U.S. Supreme Court affirmed that Secular Humanism is a religion in the Torcaso v. Watkins case (367 US 488 [1961]) when it wrote: "...among religions in this country which do not teach what would generally be considered a belief in the existence of God are Buddhism, Taoism, Ethical Culture, Secular Humanism, and others."

66. Reprinted from *Humanist Manifestos I and II*. Copyright 1973. With permission of Prometheus Books, Buffalo, New York.

67. *Free Inquiry* (Fall 1983): 10.

68. William J. Bennett, *The Index of Leading Cultural Indicators*, (Simon & Schuster, New York, 1994), 8.

69. Titus Livy, *The Early History of Rome* (Baltimore, Maryland; Penguin Books, 1960. Translation by Aubrey deSelincourt), 18.

70. Randy Phillips, "Now is the Time," *Men of Action* newsletter of Promise Keepers, Winter, 1994, 1.

71. Benjamin Franklin, *Works of the Late Doctor Benjamin Franklin Consisting of His Life, Written by Himself, Together with Essays, Humorous, Moral & Literary, Chiefly in the Manner of the Spectator,* Richard Price, ed. (Dublin: P. Wogan, P. Byrne, J. Moore, and W. Jones, 1793), 289.

# Index